101 IDEAS FOR DOWNSTAIRS

Published by BBC Books
BBC Worldwide Ltd, Woodlands,
80 Wood Lane, London W12 0TT

First published for
Marks & Spencer in 2003
This edition published in 2005
Reprinted 2005, 2006
Copyright © BBC Worldwide 2003

All photographs © *BBC Good Homes* magazine 2003

ISBN 0 563 52252 6

Edited by Joanna Simmons

Commissioning Editor: Vivien Bowler
Project Editor: Sarah Emsley
Series Design: Claire Wood
Book Design: Kathryn Gammon
Design Managers: Sarah Ponder and Annette Peppis
Production Controller: Christopher Tinker

Set in Amasis MT and ITC Officina Sans
Printed and bound in Italy by LEGO SpA
Colour origination by Butler & Tanner

101 IDEAS FOR DOWNSTAIRS

KITCHEN, DINING, LIVING

Julie Savill

BBC GoodHomes

CONTENTS

INTRODUCTION

Nothing much comes close to the sense of satisfaction you get when a friend walks into your home and falls in love with it. And, while you should always decorate to please yourself, surely being relaxed and happy in your home involves creating spaces where your friends and family are going to feel at ease and welcome.

The downstairs rooms of your house are likely to be the hardest working of all and first and foremost need to serve the day-to-day needs of your family – so you might need to consider child- or pet-proof colours and materials. But, since these rooms also double as places to entertain, you'll want bags of storage so you can sweep away the clutter when friends call, as well as flexible lighting that lets you change the mood in a flash.

Before the first lick of paint goes on the wall you should really consider your lifestyle and what use you currently make of your space. There is, for instance, no point in having a dining room if it gets used for one big meal each Christmas then simply serves as a dumping ground for the next 11 months. Far better to invest in a neat folding dining table and chairs which can be whipped out at a moment's notice and instead create a playroom for the kids, a cosy TV room, a study… Perhaps taking down the wall between sitting room and dining room to make one large space would be best if you have small rooms and a large family. Or opening up the kitchen and dining room to create an all-purpose cooking, eating, home-work and informal entertaining area. The options are almost endless but these changes are not wildly expensive (certainly cheaper than moving house!) and a little lateral thinking at this stage can sometimes transform your home completely.

Once you've got the space sorted it's time for the really pleasurable, creative bit: deciding on floor plans, colour schemes, decorating ideas and finishing touches. In this book we have pulled together 101 of the very best ideas for kitchens, dining rooms, sitting rooms and hallways to make an indispensable ideas source book that you can come back to time and time again for inspiration. Each room has its own section and contains a wide variety of styles to cater for every taste, each with a full explanation of how and why the scheme works and great tips on recreating the look for yourself at home. Simple!

Julie Savill, Editor
BBC Good Homes magazine

The look: This small kitchen has a light, spacious feel thanks to a soft palette of blues and lots of carefully planned storage space. The fridge and microwave are hidden away inside specially designed units to make the room feel less cluttered, while an open shelf along one wall means there's still enough on show to give the room character.

Colour: Blue can be a cold colour, but lighter tones are just right for creating a fresh, airy feel. Here, a deep turquoise has been used for the unit doors with a lighter blue painted on the walls. Mosaic tiles in matching tones with hints of green mixed in make a colourful, coordinated splashback.

Units: These stylish units are simplicity itself. Smooth, smart and modern, they have discreet metal handles that look equally contemporary. Their vibrant colour gives them mountains of style. The original units have been treated with a multi-surface primer and then painted. To maximize storage space, open shelving has been made from MDF and hung on an empty wall.

Splashback: Mosaics look great as a splashback and, because they're sold on square meshes, they're easy to lay and very versatile – it's not hard to get mosaics to fit narrow spaces, whereas tiles need careful cutting. They come in hundreds of colours so it's simple to find a shade that exactly suits your kitchen.

Accessories: White china with a blue line pattern tones in perfectly with this kitchen, which is important as some of the china is stored on open shelves. Glass storage jars look great and make it easy to tell when you're running low on staples. A good idea is to stick a label on the base of each jar and pencil on the food's sell-by date – once packaging has been thrown out, it's hard to remember how old your food is.

The look: A clean scheme of white and wood with splashes of red gives this room a light, airy feel. Its generous proportions mean there's plenty of storage space and its smart, streamlined look and double oven make it perfect for entertaining.

Colour: Pale colours are just the job if you want to lighten the look of your kitchen. Here, white is used, but pastels also work well. Too much white can look bleached out, so a solid beech worktop and a bamboo floor give warmth and definition while red tea towels, tins and accessories spice up the scheme.

Floor: This floor is bamboo, an eco-friendly choice since it's a grass and no natural hardwood trees are cut down to produce it. Thanks to a complex root system, bamboo grows fast and replenishes itself vigorously, so it's a true sustainable resource.

It's also perfect for a kitchen as it is resistant to scuffing, staining and damage from moisture. Here, its polished finish bounces light upwards, helping the room to feel sunny and spacious.

Oven: Two double ovens are installed side by side in this kitchen with a gas hob on top. It's a luxury only a large kitchen can afford, but ideal if you have the space and are a serious cook. Another solution would be to fit a large, range style cooker, but two conventional ovens together offer more versatility and can work out less pricey.

Splashback: White square tiles can look a little plain, so for a touch more interest, opt for rectangular ones. They're inexpensive, keep the fresh white theme but add interest to these deep splashbacks. They're tiled with white grout for a pure, fresh look.

CONTEMPORARY

The look: This is a smart, functional kitchen with plenty of space for eating, cooking and relaxing. The soft colour scheme is easy to live with but fresh and contemporary, while the open shelving creates room to have favourite pieces on show.

Colour: There is lots of colour in this room, but it's muted and gentle and adds personality to the space. A soft green on the units is teamed with chalky white walls and open shelves in duck-egg blue. These tones are livened up with flashes of shiny chrome and bold, stripy fabric on the blind and chairs.

Units: To make the most of this long room, the units have been laid out in a U shape, creating a defined kitchen and dining area. Unit doors are plain and unadorned, and this helps keep the room feeling streamlined.

It also means the backs of the units, which are clearly visible from the table, look similar to the front and just as stylish. Long shiny handles add a nice contemporary touch.

Shelves: In a big kitchen where there's plenty of space for floor units, keep wall units to a minimum or fit open shelves. These create space for storage jars and books, which add interest as well as being ready to hand when you need them. The shelves are also fitted with downlighters that provide useful light to the worktop.

Splashback: Glass makes a stunning splashback and allows the wall colour to show through. Ask a glazier to cut a piece to fit, and make sure you use toughened glass that can withstand the heat from the hob rings.

The look: A modern mix of cool cream and chocolate brown gives this kitchen oodles of class. The units are perfectly pared down and discreet, and a mix of ethnic-looking accessories lend the room an African feel.

Colour: A scheme of brown and cream has been stuck to rigidly in this room, making it streamlined and smart. It's far from boring though – the colours may be limited, but pattern and texture is not. The plates on the walls, and the baskets, pots and storage jars all add interest and lift the room from simple to super stylish.

Floor: There's a dark wooden floor in this kitchen that is easy to keep clean. The boards have been varnished to protect them from the inevitable kitchen spills and this makes them hard wearing, too. To add some pattern, a rug has been laid under the table and chairs, positioned well away from the worktops to avoid crumbs or mess landing on it.

Worktop: Inexpensive, simple units are given a shot of luxury with a Corian worktop. Corian is an incredibly tough composite material that can't be marked, scored or stained. It can be made to any shape or size and comes in hundreds of different colours. The only downside? It's very expensive, but worth considering in a small kitchen or one where the minimum has been spent on units. Here, a thin strip has also been fitted along the wall as a splashback, helping the room feel coordinated.

Accessories: Kitchen clutter is tidied away into cupboards leaving a shelf and surfaces clear for decorative pieces that are key to this room's success. A wall-mounted basket is a great plant holder, while the patterned plates and shapely vases and pots add to the African feel.

The look: This is a colourful, welcoming kitchen, with plenty of space to cook, sit and eat, making it a sociable and enjoyable place to be. A mix of green, cream and warm wood create a sunny feel, while plenty of china and stainless steel add sparkle and pattern.

Colour: Kitchens can take a strong colour because there's not usually a whole wall of it on show, just patches between units. Here, a lime green has been painted on the walls and the colour has been picked up in the tiles. To create contrast, a mix of green and cream tiles have been used. Birch units add a sunny glow while the blind, china and plants weave in splashes of blue, yellow and yet more green. Even though the overall effect is vibrant, the scheme actually only sticks to three chief shades – green, cream and wood – which prevents the room looking hectic and uncoordinated.

Units: To make the most of the space, the wall units have been designed to angle around the room's corners. This softens hard lines and helps the space feel relaxed. Open shelves create a space for displaying favourite china, while doors with frosted glass insets add texture and lighten the look.

Floor: The floor tiles are calico coloured and discreetly shaded so they won't show every mark or scuff. This is a bonus in a kitchen, where spills and splashes often occur and lots of traffic passes through.

Oven: The modern double oven and hood are made from stainless steel. This is matched by the finish on the handles, while the pans, utensil rail and sink all tie in, too.

The look: This simply stylish room has all the hallmarks of a well-planned modern kitchen: neat units; a smart built-in oven; a touch of colour; and clutter kept to a minimum to help the room feel larger.

Colour: Pale birch units have been sanded and primed and then painted with a lilac satinwood in the centre of each door. This soft, airy shade gives the room some interest without closing it in, and it's picked up on the walls for a coordinated look. Colour like this can easily be updated, whereas patterned tiles and flooring are more permanent. The pale laminate floor tones in perfectly with the birch of the units and the light worktop, so the room feels large and harmonious.

Units: These pale birch units are simple and modern, with neat rounded handles that look stylish but unobtrusive. They've been painted to update their look and give them a dash more style, and can be painted over at any time to change the feel of the room.

Lighting: A ledge has been constructed around the room, slightly lower than the ceiling, for the spotlighting to be fixed in. Downlighters shine directly onto the sink and worktops. This provides essential task lighting – light that helps with specific jobs – making cooking and preparing food easier and safer.

Accessories: A favourite print, in a frame that matches the units, creates a focal point. With all but essential kitchen kit and gadgets tidied away in cupboards, the worktops are clear for jars of pasta, tea and coffee. This is practical – it's good to have them to hand – and looks great, too.

CONTEMPORARY

The look: Clean modern lines and fresh colours mix with a few classic touches to give this kitchen a smart twist on contemporary style.

Colour: Choosing coloured units is a great way to bring some va va voom to your kitchen. Here, warm, lemony yellow units have been fitted and teamed with yellow walls for a fresh feel. To rev up the colour still more, bright tiles in orange, black and grey make a zingy splashback and tone in with a colourful patterned blind. Terracotta tiles and a wooden worktop anchor the scheme with their natural tones and bring some subtle warmth.

Units: These look sleek and modern, and are great value buys from a large DIY store. The doors have a slightly Shaker feel, but the long metal handles keep the look modern. Appliances are integrated to keep the room feeling neat and sleek, while the dishwasher is semi integrated, so the control panel is still on display and easy to get at.

Sink: Butler's sinks bring a touch of old country style to any kitchen and are really popular today. Remember that you'll need slightly more room to install one than a conventional sink and you shouldn't integrate it, or you won't see its sleek enamel side. They're great for washing big pans because of their size, but can be chipped so be careful when washing large items. A swan necked mixer tap looks great – another old-world touch – and its height means it won't get in the way when you're washing up.

Blind: Kitchen windowsills tend to work hard, often crammed with bits and bobs, so a Roman blind is perfect – you can draw it down as far as your accessories will allow. This one looks neat and adds another shot of warm colour to the room, helping it feel inviting and nicely offsetting all that yellow.

CONTEMPORARY

The look: Bright and light, this is a kitchen guaranteed to lift your spirits. Simple white units look fresh and clean while a stainless-steel range cooker means business for the serious cook. Stylish accessories and a few plants add to the fresh, relaxed feel – a contemporary look that's friendly, too.

Colour: The mood is light and easy in this room, so dark colours are out. Instead, a pale blue creates an uplifting, outdoorsy feel and teams perfectly with the white units, shiny handles and frosted glass doors. The wooden flooring adds warmth, toning in with the dark wood-effect worktops.

Units: These units are great-value basics from one of the large DIY stores, leaving money spare to splurge on the range cooker. The long chrome handles ooze contemporary cool, while the frosted glass insets on the cupboard doors keep the room feeling light and stop them looking boring or too uniform.

Splashback: Large white tiles make up the splashback here, chosen for their unfussy look and light-reflecting properties. Big tiles give a sleeker look than small ones and create a really glossy effect that's perfect for this airy, bright room. A shelf runs across the top of the tiles, bridging the gap between the units and creating display space for plants.

Accessories: This kitchen is no shrine to minimalism. It gets its character from the interesting pieces dotted around the room. A huge clock looks dramatic, while potted plants look fresh and pretty. A blackboard is really useful in a kitchen – great for scrawling shopping lists on or keeping up with the family's comings and goings.

CONTEMPORARY

The look: Colour and pattern combine here to create a kitchen with a mix of features. Cool white units are classically shaped and chequer-board tiles look timeless, while orange walls and a pink fireplace inject some family-friendly fun.

Colour: This spacious room is enlivened with hot orange and pink. Orange on the walls tones in nicely with the pale wood flooring and worktops, while the fireplace's old tiles have been painted shocking pink to give them a whole new look. The white units help lighten the effect of the two bright colours and lots of pale laminate flooring creates a soothing, neutral base.

Units: These are a classic, Shaker-feel design, with wood-effect sides to break up the white. There's an in-built wine rack, a plate rack and open shelving, which creates a place for everything, while a shapely wooden border runs above and below the open shelves adding decorative detail.

Floor: A pale wood-effect laminate is the flooring in this room. Laminate is relatively inexpensive, easy to lay and, treated right, hard wearing. Because it's made by bonding (laminating) a thin strip of wood-effect material to boards, it has to be protected from water which can cause the two layers to warp and come unstuck. So, although it is suitable for a kitchen, it's a good idea to mop up any spills as soon as they happen.

Fireplace: The fireplace in this kitchen has been made a focal point and it provides space for displaying favourite pieces on the mantelpiece. A shelf above adds more display space, while the fire surround's old-fashioned tiles have been painted with two coats of tile primer, then covered with pink paint to give them a contemporary edge.

CONTEMPORARY

The look: Pristine white units, unvarnished beech-block worktops, a shiny sink and taps, and smart chrome power points combine to create a fuss-free contemporary kitchen.

Colour: A long window takes up one wall of this kitchen, flooding it with light. To make the most of this, the walls are painted a soft, off-white shade, which also helps create a sense of space in what is a fairly compact kitchen. White units further increase the airy feel while soft green mosaics with a border of black make a chic splashback with colour that warms up the room. Vinyl flooring in a dark, slate grey ties in with the black mosaic and anchors the whole scheme.

Units: These are beautifully understated. White laminate doors with small, unfussy handles are elegantly plain and discreet. To help the room feel as big as possible, there are no wall units. A run of neat wooden shelves have been fitted instead, providing space for both storage and display.

Worktop: The units are given a shot of warmth by the worktop which is made from solid, unvarnished beech block sealed with linseed oil for a low-sheen finish. Solid wood worktops like this need looking after – re-oil every year to protect the wood and keep it looking tip top.

Sockets: Finishing touches can make a huge difference to the impact of a kitchen. Here, grubby plastic sockets and switches have been swapped for stylish chrome fittings with a woven effect – smart, simple and perfectly in keeping with the room's contemporary feel.

The look: Tucked up in the eaves, this kitchen is low on ceiling height but high on style. Soft lilac and pale wood units team well together and create a subtle, stylish look. A dark worktop adds some contrast and definition, while baskets break up the cupboards and add character.

Colour: In a small kitchen like this, it's a good idea to use no more than three colours as more can make the space look cluttered and busy. Here, lilac has been painted on to the walls and ceiling to match the tiles. This creates a continuous sweep making it hard for the eye to tell where the ceiling starts. As a result, the steep angle is less obvious and the room feels bigger. Pale wooden units are matched by pale laminate flooring, while the black worktop ties in well with the steely appliances and pans and adds some useful definition to the pale scheme.

Units: Pale wooden units help make even the smallest room bigger, and sexy handles with a textured design give them an extra shot of style. Two basket drawers add further character to this tiny room without sacrificing storage space or interrupting the streamlined effect. A black granite-effect worktop is perfect here, a welcome note of dark colour that perfectly divides the lilac and pale wood colours and gives the small room impact.

Accessories: In a little kitchen, it's important to keep bits-and-bobs stored out of sight or the room can feel cluttered and even smaller. A few storage jars and the odd essential bottle of oil are on show, but otherwise workspace is left clear for preparing and serving food.

CONTEMPORARY

The look: Clean, crisp and contemporary, this kitchen is a modern classic. Neat white units provide plenty of storage space, bold blue walls add a dash of drama, and pretty mosaics make a watertight, practical splashback.

Colour: White units are classics of the contemporary kitchen world, and they won't date either. They instantly make a room feel bigger and more open, and can be teamed with almost any wall colour. Here, a rich blue has been used to invigorate the walls and a splashback of coloured mosaics, which range from deepest navy near the worksurface to fresh turquoise at the top, looks super stylish.

Units: The high ceilings in this kitchen have been made the most of with a versatile mix of vertical and horizontal units. Space that is often wasted is made use of here – there's a skinny drawer beneath the oven. The addition of glass insets in a couple of the unit doors breaks up the look, giving it pace and interest, while the handles add chunky style to the plain doors.

Floor: The floor is laminate but, rather than the usual wood effect, it has a metallic grey finish. This tones in perfectly with the handles and appliances, keeping the room looking chicly modern and beautifully coordinated.

Window: The large window lets in lots of light and is a real asset in this room. Curtains would look too fussy here – all wrong for a simple, modern scheme. Instead, a neat, grey venetian blind has been hung to offer privacy without obstructing light. It hangs just the length of the window so it doesn't cover the radiator and stop heat from flowing into the room.

The look: Bright, zingy and cheerful, the colours in this room make a bold statement. Maple units add a warm glow, but it's the bold tiles and blind that first catch the eye – guaranteed to wake you up in the morning.

Colour: The patterned blind in lime green and navy was the inspiration for the room's colour scheme. A matching green has been painted on the walls, while tiles in a mix of yellow, navy and turquoise have been used to create a knock-'em-dead splashback. The black worktop helps calm everything down, providing a deep matt finish to divide the vibrant tiles from the warm wood.

Units: The units are in soft, honey-coloured maple, giving the room a glow without being too dark. The design is super simple, so the beautiful graining on the wood becomes the key feature. Rounded brushed steel handles add a contemporary note and match the brim of the oven.

Splashback: Bright-as-you-like tiles have been used to create a high splashback around the room. The colours run diagonally to give the scheme some order, but a random pattern would look just as good. Before you fit tiles like this, be sure you really love them. If you tire of the colour, tiles can be complicated and expensive to change.

Accessories: For an all-out colourful look, the china matches the tiles and blind. This says that the owners are confident and passionate about the colour scheme they've chosen. They love it, and they want the whole room to tie in with it. It's a bold look, but it's been pulled off perfectly here.

The look: Cool and classic, this stylish kitchen is full of clever ideas that help maximize its space and boost its light.

Units: Fresh white units with neat round handles give this room plenty of understated style. The units were bought unfinished and then primed and painted to help keep costs down. To make the most of the dead space underneath the base units, drawers were fitted. Rather than fitting wall units the owners decided to sacrifice the storage to avoid overcrowding the space. Wall units either side of the window would have also reduced the amount of light and compromised the airy feel.

Worktop: A gorgeous curved granite worktop gives this kitchen serious sex appeal. It takes away all the hard edges, leading the eye around the room. It is also extended up the wall behind the hob to make a splashback and is used on the windowsill. Small kitchens like this can look very boxy, but this cleverly side steps that problem. Although expensive, granite is extremely hardworking and heat resistant, plus its cool feel makes it ideal for cooking on – pastry in particular benefits from a cold worksurface.

Cooker: A smart stainless-steel oven, hob and hood give the room up-to-date glamour and make cooking a breeze. To keep the stainless-steel feel, brushed steel power points have been installed. Bear in mind that details like this can make a huge difference to the overall effect, particularly in a small room where everything is more noticeable.

The look: This L-shaped kitchen is elegant and stylish with lots of pretty details set against a unified, clean backdrop. Wooden units, granite-look worktops and slate-effect floor tiles create a subtle mix of colour and texture and form the key ingredients for this good-looking room.

Colour: The walls have been washed with a soft, chalky emulsion paint to tie in with neutral splashback tiles with a slightly textured surface. The floor breaks away from the palette of pale neutrals. Its slate effect is mottled with amber which grounds the scheme and matches both the units and appliances.

Units: Simply styled with small round handles and a raised border on the doors, these pale oak units are elegant and stylish. The granite-effect laminate worktop adds freckly colour and keeps the look light. The cabinets are arranged in an L shape, with the wall units kept to one side of the room to help enhance the feeling of space and give an open, airy feel. The sink is positioned under the window, so there's a view for the poor soul on washing-up duty.

Appliances: Appliances in this room are not integrated, but left on show. In silver finishes or with brushed metal trims, they look good and stop the kitchen from feeling too uniform. They also tone in well with the worktops and flooring, adding interest and keeping the room feeling coordinated.

Window: A Roman blind in soft woven linen adds privacy but is unfussy and minimal. Fitting it above the window recess means it can then be lowered without knocking the plants on the windowsill or disturbing anything else placed there.

The look: Creamy units with a nod to country style are teamed with a modern oven, warm red walls and plenty of eye-catching stainless-steel accessories.

Colour: The units and tiles are a soft, warm cream, creating an easy-to-live-with base. Red and green, in equally soft tones, have been painted on the walls to give the room warmth, while stainless-steel and chrome gadgets and utensils add sparkle that lifts the whole room.

Units: Units in every shape and size have been fitted here to make the most of a small space. Small cupboards, like the ones either side of the hood, obviously don't hold as much as big ones, but they're perfect for storing small kitchen essentials such as spice jars and tins that can be hard to find, getting easily shunted to the back of bigger cupboards. Open shelves, painted on the inside in the same red as the walls, make use of the narrow space adjoining the hood and create storage space with a place to show off favourite finds.

Worktop: This dark, granite-effect laminate adds some definition to the room. It's a good choice in any room because it's a way to introduce dark colour and create a strong line between units, without making the room feel gloomy.

Wall rack: To squeeze every ounce of usefulness out of a small kitchen space, think about hanging a wall rack like this one. It makes use of a small space where a unit wouldn't fit and provides vital storage space, with utensils hanging to hand at all times.

The look: This spacious room has its original pine floorboards, which create a wonderful wood glow at floor level and are a key feature of the room. Units have been carefully chosen to complement them while a huge range cooker gives this family room a professional edge.

Colour: Plenty of natural light floods in from the large French doors at the end of the room. To maximize this, and to help the space feel extra bright and airy, the walls have been painted pure brilliant white. The colour comes from the wood, the china and the garden which is clearly visible from any part of the room.

Units: Space and storage aren't a problem in a large room like this. The units were chosen for their streamlined feel, to help open up the space and to keep the focus on the garden beyond. To stop the room from feeling overwhelmed with wood, two tones which complement each other were chosen – the pale wood-effect of the units and the solid beech worktop match the pine boards perfectly.

Appliances: Ultra modern stainless-steel appliances and accessories team well with wooden furniture and flooring, as long as the units are modern and streamlined too. This professional range gives the room cooking clout, its long handles matching those on the unit doors. The huge Fifties-style fridge freezer is a real asset. Stylish enough to stand alone, it adds to the room's chic, loft feel.

Floor: Original pine boards have been sanded down and varnished, turning them a warm colour and adding a slight sheen that helps bounce light around the room. The varnish also protects the wood from splashes and spills – essential in a kitchen.

The look: Cool cream is brightened with warm blue for a stylish but liveable look. Shaker-style units and a ceramic Belfast sink are kitchen classics, but teamed here with up-to-date flooring and some smart accessories, they get a fresh, new direction.

Colour: A cool, cream kitchen and neutral off-white paintwork create a warm base, which is lifted with a smart deep-blue linen blind. For added impact, vases along the windowsill in matching shades of blue and cream extend the colour scheme to every aspect of the room.

Units: The cream Shaker-style units keep the room feeling light and have a more homely edge than plain, contemporary units. They're given even more style by a solid wood worktop – an expensive option, but very beautiful and just right in a comfortable, warm-looking room like this.

Sink: Adding a traditional ceramic Belfast sink gives the room further homely plus points. Ceramic sinks have an old-style charm and, because they're not built into a worktop like a steel sink generally is, you can see one side and get a pleasing sense of their solidity. They also help break up a run of units. This sink has been given a contemporary lift with a stylish brushed-nickel mixer tap.

Noticeboard: The back of the L-shaped units is the perfect height for a child-sized noticeboard. To make it, a strip of magnetic paint and then a blue top coat has been applied to the unit backs.

The look: This kitchen is big on space and style. There's miles of worktop to prepare food, acres of storage space, and lots of colour and interest to woo even the most reluctant of cooks.

Colour: Classic beech units and cream walls create a warm, neutral backdrop for this kitchen, but to liven it up, a tongue-and-groove splashback has been painted bright orange, and blue units are dotted between the pale ones. The worktop has a high gloss finish that further boosts the room's colour, while bright plates hanging in a rack do the rest.

Units: Simple and stylish, these beech units get a chic lift with extra long handles that break them up and create graphic lines. To further pep up the look, blue cupboard doors have been added on a couple of units. It's a subtle but really effective trick, adding interest and pace without spoiling the room's harmonious feel. Walls are kept mostly free, with only one unit fitted. This is a feature in itself as, rather than being wall hung, it stretches right down to the worktop. It also has a glass inset in the door to keep it looking light.

Splashback: Wooden tongue-and-groove panelling has been used as a splashback here, painted orange to add colour. A gloss paint was used so the wood is watertight, which also adds shine and keeps the room feeling fresh.

Hob and hood: Both the hob and hood are on a big scale, but they can afford to be since the room is so spacious. They suit the dimensions and give this kitchen a professional edge – this room doesn't just look good, it works hard too.

The look: Colour is king in this bright and welcoming kitchen. Orange walls, deep honey-coloured pine units and lush blue tiles look stunning together and give this room a show-stopping personality.

Colour: Bright shades like these are not for the fainthearted, but they give this room life and energy. The kitchen is one of the few rooms in the house where strong colour often works really well – units break up wall space so you're rarely confronted with a whole wall of colour. Here, the orange ties in well with the deep, honey-coloured pine units. Blue tiles that are as bold as the orange add more impact – pale tiles here might be dominated by the walls.

Units: Pine units shout country style. These have a simple grooved design and white porcelain knobs with a crackle glaze that go well with the butler's sink. An island unit provides plenty of work and storage space and gives the room a free-flowing feel.

Tiles: These big, rustic-looking blue tiles suit this room beautifully. A mix of dark and light tiles have been used to add a bit of interest and their surfaces are nicely uneven – a rustic plus point. Using tiles as a work-surface has many advantages. They're heat resistant, easy to lay and good for chopping on. Remember, though, that white grout can get dirty easily and tiles may crack if you bang heavy pans down on them.

The look: Simple units in fresh white are teamed with stripped, painted floorboards to make a clean, blank canvas. Added to this are lots of pretty country-style accessories, which add interest and colour.

Colour: The colours are fresh and bright in this kitchen. White units and appliances, pale blue-washed floorboards and clean white walls make a simple, light, space-enhancing combination. Colour comes from the pretty pots, canisters and bowls dotted around. The pale blue of the boards is also picked up on the retro-style fridge, which adds a dash more pastel colour to the room.

Units: These units are simple and unfussy and so help the room feel bigger. They bring a touch of country style without disturbing the simplicity of the scheme. Open shelves at the end of a run of units make use of space that would be too small for a separate cupboard. They also provide space to show off favourite china.

Floor: Old original boards have been painted a powder blue to make a pretty but practical floor. You can buy specialist floor paints in lots of colours these days, or simply apply a couple of coats of emulsion then seal with a tough acrylic varnish. Just remember that any pale floor shows up marks and crumbs easily, so will need more attention than dark boards would do.

Accessories: A lovely combination of pieces gives this room bags of country style. The old clock adds a retro shot to plain walls, while shapely bowls and blue and white china shout rustic style. The old metal bread tin is another key country ingredient. You can scout around second-hand markets for an original, but many shops now sell them.

The look: There's a pleasingly ramshackle look to this kitchen, with plenty to draw the eye. There's lots of colour and tons of rustic charm, delivered wholesale by the massive four-oven Aga. Door-less units mean kitchen essentials are on show and wall space has been maximized with several rails and metal shelves.

Colour: With the vast black Aga dominating the room, the walls and units have been painted a soft creamy green to lighten the look. Pale flooring helps bounce light upwards, while red fabric in place of a unit door adds a bold splash of colour, picked up and matched by various colourful pots, pans and fridge magnets displayed around the room.

Storage: The huge Aga takes up most of the space in this kitchen, leaving little room for units. The few simple wooden units have been painted a soft green and, to make more storage space, every available stretch of wall has been fitted with shelves, rails or plate racks. To squeeze even more storage potential out of the metal shelves, S-shaped hooks are hung off them, providing a place to hang utensils, mugs and pans. Far from making the room feel cluttered, this suits its colourful country look and adds mountains of character. A freestanding butcher's block is a good extension to the worksurface and provides more storage and hanging rails beneath.

Floor: Beech laminate has been laid here, an inexpensive and stylish option. It's easy to keep clean – just brush and wipe down with a slightly moist cloth – and creates a light, neutral backdrop for the action above.

The look: There's a relaxed, lived-in look to this kitchen which makes it welcoming and informal. Chunky units painted warm colours, a giant range and warm wooden flooring combine to create an unfitted, freestanding feel.

Colour: The soft cream of the walls teamed with the rich, earthy red of the units instantly creates a country feel. Dark wooden flooring and a large dining table tone in beautifully while the deep grey of the slate splashback adds another natural, rustic shade.

Units: Although actually built-in, the chunky, unfussy style of these large units gives them a relaxed, free-standing look. The simple tongue-and-groove wood looks nicely rural and the doors are hung on large black hinges – another rustic touch. The home-built units are deeper than usual, creating acres of storage space inside and a wide worksurface, perfect when worktop space is at a premium.

Oven: If you love to cook, a professional-style range like this is unbeatable. With massive oven space, numerous rings and a powerful extractor it's a hard-working addition to a serious kitchen. It also makes quite a centrepiece, suiting a room with big dimensions that is not the familiar galley shape – a large cooker would look wildly out of proportion in a small, narrow room.

Splashback: Using slate as a splashback is unusual, but suits this rustic room perfectly. Slate is heatproof, so works well here, but it's also heavy so you need to get expert advice about fixing it to a wall. Be sure to wipe up splashes when they happen as slate is slightly porous and could mark.

COUNTRY

The look: This room combines country classics – like a Rayburn oven, a hanging rack laden with pots, and lots of wicker storage baskets – with up-to-date touches, such as the stylish floor and hip artwork, for a modern country look.

Colour: The rich red Rayburn has dictated the room's colour scheme. A fresh blue has been teamed with it, while go-with-anything white units add freshness. The swish pebble-effect floor has warm blue, grey and reddish notes mixed in it – a perfect match.

Units: Simple white units with a tongue-and-groove finish and a rich wooden worktop look stylish and unfussy in this room. Rounded handles lend an old-style feel that keeps the room feeling country rather than contemporary, while open shelves provide space for wicker storage baskets, another rustic touch.

Floor: The pebble floor tiles are super stylish and unusual. They add a quirky, modern note to this room, but still tie in perfectly with its main ingredients. Made from tough, water-resistant vinyl, they also make a very practical choice in a room that's subject to lots of activity and mess.

Hanging rack: In a kitchen that's short on space, the trick is to make use of otherwise redundant surfaces. If the walls are covered with units, but storage space is still short, try a hanging rack like this one. Securely fixed to the ceiling, it provides a place for heaps of pots and pans, freeing up vital cupboard space for food, china and glassware.

There's
no mistaking a Pollock.
It has genius
splashed all over it.

The look: There's a rustic, shabby-chic feel to this kitchen. Deep drawers, panelled doors and lots of open shelving give it plenty of personality, while a distressed table and chairs provide a place for meals and boost the informal feel.

Colour: There's a blue and cream theme to this room. The units and wall panelling are a rich grey blue, brighter blue tiles add a fresh feel while blue chairs and table with battered paintwork bring personality. Cream walls above the panelling and a pale floor stop the room from feeling gloomy and create a soft, warm contrast.

Units: These units were built to fit around a few key pieces – the old butler's sink and the big range style cooker. Their panelled finish matches the walls, helping them blend in, while deep drawers have a nice, old dresser feel.

Shelves: Modern kitchens tend to hide everything away, but storing kitchen kit on open shelves is a classic element of a country kitchen. Here, a rail beneath the shelves means utensils are also hung to hand, while plates are stacked in piles or stored in the built-in rack, creating an informal, higgledy-piggledy effect that's the essence of country style.

Table and chairs: These cute little chairs, found at a car-boot sale, have woven seats and distressed paintwork, so they look like they've seen many years of active service – perfect for this kitchen's laid-back look. The table has the same feel, its battered paint giving it real character and its small size is just right for this compact room.

The look: Colourful, characterful and brimming with personality, this rustic kitchen was cleverly put together with reclaimed finds and lots of imagination.

Colour: Yellow, cream and green make a vibrant, sunny combination in this room and a little varnished wood has been thrown in to add country-style warmth. Cream on the shutters, and an even softer cream on the walls, cool the look down. The room's high ceilings and spaciousness mean the colour doesn't shrink the space, it invigorates it.

Units: These units were made and fitted by a carpenter, a great way to get exactly the style you want, and often cheaper than buying from a kitchen retailer. The tongue-and-groove doors have been painted a grassy green and fitted with a random collection of knobs for a simple, rustic look. Rather than fill the high walls with units, a thin shelf has been created for storage space. It frames the wall and the pots that hang within it. This rustic, informal look is brought bang up-to-date with a modern oven and cooker hood.

Sink: An old butler's sink takes pride of place here. You can pick these up at salvage yards or fairs, often fully repaired and ready for installation. If you like the style but prefer the comfort of buying a new product, many bathroom and kitchen retailers now sell authentic repro designs. Although sinks like this look handsome, they're generally deeper and wider than a conventional sink so they take up more room and take longer to fill. It is also much easier to break glasses or china against their surface, which is far less forgiving than modern stainless steel.

The look: This stylish, modern kitchen combines plain doors with soft colour to create a contemporary effect. Good quality taps, accessories and splashback give the room a classy edge, even though the units are fronted with inexpensive MDF doors.

Colour: Soft blue is an easy-to-live-with shade that gives this plain and simple kitchen heaps of style. A slightly paler blue than the units has been painted on the walls to create a little depth and glass splashbacks have been fixed in place, allowing the colour to be seen while adding a little sparkle. White, chrome and plum accessories lift the look and a wooden worktop adds warmth, which is important as some shades of blue can be cold.

Units: An inexpensive way to revamp a tired kitchen is to remove the doors and replace them with MDF ones. You can get MDF cut to fit at a wood merchants or DIY store. You can probably use the existing hinges to fix them in place, then just paint them whatever shade you like. Super-plain doors like these don't have to look boring. The combination of colour and some long, sexy handles makes them look chic and contemporary.

Splashback: Glass makes an ideal splashback. It's watertight, easy to clean and looks more discreet than tiles, helping a room feel light and airy. Ask a glazier to cut laminated glass to size then simply fix it in place using mirror screws.

Flooring: This unusual flooring is actually a pale teak laminate. It works perfectly here, adding warmth while still toning in with the pale blue scheme. Laminate is far less expensive than solid wood flooring and comes in a huge variety of finishes – ideal for a modern, budget kitchen.

The look: This kitchen started life as bland but functional. With a few clever tricks, it was transformed into this colourful, super-stylish room where modern meets retro.

Colour: Strong colours in a kitchen are nothing to fear – use them with lots of white and you can't go wrong. What were once grey units have been primed and then painted with bright green satinwood paint. To offset them, and for maximum clean appeal, the walls have been painted white and white vinyl flooring has been laid underfoot.

Worktops: Stainless-steel worktops look modern and industrial. They're tough and heat resistant so you can put pots straight down on them, but they can be scored by cutting directly onto them and greasy fingers tend to leave marks. Stainless steel is best kept clean with a soft, rather than an abrasive cloth and wiped over with a little baby oil once in a while to bring up the shine. These worktops were actually sent away to be re-covered in stainless steel – a clever way to update existing surfaces.

Splashback: To give the room loads of character and stop it feeling too sterile, a splashback with a crazy paving feel has been made by cutting ceramic tiles into triangles and rectangles and then sticking them onto the wall in a random pattern. Be careful though, the grout needs to be flush with the tiles, as edges may be sharp.

Accessories: The worktops have been left clutter-free so that the stainless steel can be admired (and kept in pristine condition). Just a few, carefully chosen pieces, such as the Fifties-feel blue toaster and attractive, old-style weighing scales enhance the overall look, and work with the clean lines and fresh colour scheme.

The look: Warm, rustic and simple, this kitchen got its great new look on the tightest of budgets. Doors were clad, walls painted and smart new handles added to completely change its feel.

Units: Covering up tired old units can be just as effective as replacing them and it's an awful lot cheaper. Here, lengths of tongue-and-groove have been fixed over the old doors and tacked in place with thin panel pins (thick ones could make the wood split). Stylish new handles have been screwed in place to give the doors a rustic look.

Shelves: If you have space in a kitchen, open shelves that you can use as much for display as for storage are a great idea. They break up a run of units and offer a chance to show off favourite pieces, a perfect way to inject colour and personality into a room. This unit has been primed and painted with an off-white satin paint.

Splashback: It's not absolutely essential to have a splashback behind your sink taps, but it does help prevent water marking the wall and is therefore recommended. Here, a lip on the worktop extends a little way up the walls, protecting the join between wall and worktop and offering a partial shield from splashes.

Accessories: A wooden plate rack fits in perfectly with the wooden unit doors and keeps the look natural and organic. White bowls and china with a blue rim look simple and stylish, and keep the room feeling fresh, up-to-date and unfussy.

The look: Set in a Fifties flat, this kitchen has a fittingly retro feel. Bright colours, simple units and plenty of old style accessories give it a strong personality, while modern ingredients, such as the colourful juicer, add a contemporary edge.

Colour: This room gets all day sun, so it's perfect for strong, fresh colour. A bright apple green has been used to lighten and give personality, while white units and a pale blue worktop provide a contrast. Lots of colourful accessories complete the look, adding to the Fifties atmosphere.

Cooker: The trend these days is for built-in ovens and hobs, but there are lots of free-standing ovens on the market that are well styled and good looking. They also have the advantage of being portable, so you can move them around and, ultimately, take them with you when you move. This one was chosen for its retro look, just right in this room.

Units: To update this kitchen cheaply, a new worktop and door fronts have been added to the existing carcass. This is simple, quick and easy to do, and it's hundreds of pounds cheaper than installing a whole new kitchen.

Accessories: Once you've created a feel with units and wall colour, accessories can make or break a kitchen. Here, the addition of lots of colourful enamelware, Fifties-style gadgets and even a poster or two beautifully reinforces the Fifties feel of the room, adding heaps of style. Kitchen bits and bobs are squirrelled neatly away in the units to let these striking pieces shine out.

The look: In this kitchen, old units have been given a budget makeover – the original doors have been replaced with MDF and painted a soft cream. The money saved on this was invested in quality handles, a sleek stainless-steel trim for the worktop and a state-of-the-art integrated oven.

Colour: A neutral scheme of cream, grey and soft white has classic impact that softens a modern design. Inexpensive wall shelves have been painted the same cream to give the room a considered, coordinated look. A dark slate floor adds some richness, anchoring the cream and stopping the room feeling too pale.

Units: MDF was cut to fit the existing units and narrow strips of it were glued to the doors before they were painted cream. To give the doors further style and a professional finish, smart, recessed handles were fitted, while the worktop was edged with stainless steel for a classic, upmarket touch.

Window: In a room that's predominantly cream the window dressing does need to match, but using a fabric with touches of other colours in it is a good way to introduce some variety without spoiling the coordinated look. Here, an elegant Roman blind, made from quality fabric with a subtle flower pattern, introduces some soft green and mushroom tones. The horizontal lines of the blind folds also match the lines on the unit doors – a nice touch.

Splashback: This inexpensive splashback has been made by painting a thin MDF board with gloss paint. The gloss paint can be wiped down, and here the same colour as the units has been used to keep the room looking seamless.

The look: Here, an old kitchen has been given a bright and cheery makeover at very little expense. The result is a colourful space with zingy tiles, lots of eye-catching china and a Caribbean feel.

Colour: Old kitchen units have been given a lick of bright green paint to totally change their feel and bring them right up-to-date, and the strong green is picked up in the mosaic worktop. Here, sparkly tiles in white, red, blue and green add bright colour without being overbearing. Brightly painted china and jewel-bright glassware add to the mix, creating a thoroughly energizing space.

Units: Revamping old units is as cheap and easy as painting them. To help them look even more stylish, fit new handles like these shiny metal ones. If you really can't stand the style of the unit doors, you can get them replaced. Many companies offer this service but, while it's relatively inexpensive to do and far cheaper than buying a new kitchen, painting doors remains the best budget option.

Tiles: This splashback has been given a new lease of life with some paint. For a smooth, professional result like this, mask off each tile and spray rather than brush on the paint. A decorative worktop has been made by laying individual mosaics into tile adhesive, then grouting. It's fiddly work but the results are unique and very pretty.

Accessories: Old pine shelving has been used to create a handy spice rack on the wall. It has bags of style and means spices are conveniently to hand. A string of chillies looks great and is practical too. Cacti in a painted wooden box jazz up the windowsill while a wooden plate rack matches the shelf and keeps the room feeling rustic.

The look: This dining area is part of a large kitchen that is equipped with freestanding rather than fitted furniture. This creates a relaxed feel and means the dining table doesn't feel wildly out of place. Plenty of warm wood, a soft, mineral green on the walls, plus plants, woven baskets and retro accessories give the room an organic, natural feel.

Colour: Three key colours combine in this room. The warm olive green of the walls creates a soft, natural backdrop, perfect with all the golden wood that's set against it. Touches of cream add freshness without jarring or losing the soft, inspired-by-nature feel.

Furniture: The striking centrepiece of this room is a really good-quality solid wood table with matching chairs. Dining tables like this don't come cheap but, well cared for and classically shaped, they will last a lifetime and never go out of fashion. The wooden console is used here for food preparation, but when cleared of cooking paraphernalia it makes a handsome sideboard, with storage space aplenty.

Accessories: Lots of baskets are used for storage here. They're inexpensive and natural, adding texture and warm colour too. A row of succulent plants makes a beautiful table centrepiece, and, unlike cut flowers, they'll live for years. In old terracotta pots, they're a weathered foil to the exotic, highly-polished wood of the tabletop.

Fridge: Having your fridge in your dining area might not sound ideal, but if you pick a gorgeous, design classic like this Fifties-style Smeg fridge, it will look stunning anywhere. The retro styling is in keeping with this room's anti hi-tech feel, and its colour is perfect too.

The look: There's an opulent, exotic feel to this dining room thanks to the rich, strong colours on the walls and the elegant wrought-iron furniture.

Colour: Lime green and burgundy have been combined on the walls to create a dramatic, colour-rich room. They're complemented by matching green china and are teamed with a further dark shade – deep blue on the seat covers, glasses and plates. A pale wood floor introduces a note of lightness that lifts the scheme and helps it feel dramatic, rather than gloomy.

Furniture: The wrought-iron table and chairs were made to order, giving the room a unique personality. A glass top was chosen for the table to keep the room feeling light,

essential with all those dark colours. The table is also circular, which is more sociable than a rectangular design and perfect for small spaces.

Lighting: There's a metal chandelier and wall sconce in this room, carefully chosen to complement the wrought-iron table at the room's centre. A mix of overhead and wall lighting on different circuits means you can have a range of light, from bright to soft, to suit whatever you're using the room for at the time.

Accessories: These have been strictly chosen to follow the room's colour scheme. Glasses, place mats and some of the plates are deep blue to tie in with the seat covers, while the remaining china is the same vibrant lime as the walls.

The look: Fresh and zingy, this dining room is decorated in spirit-lifting shades and kitted out with simple modern pieces that are hard-wearing and versatile.

Colour: Orange creates energy and a healthy appetite so it's perfect for a dining room. Here, to create a feeling of balance, one wall has been painted orange and the other white. On the tablecloth material, mouth-watering bright citrus meets mellow yellow for a colourful rather than garish effect. There's plenty of white on hand too, to keep the room feeling fresh rather than violently bright.

Furniture: An informal mix of furniture has been combined to create a laid-back and friendly space. The simple, inexpensive table is given a shot of glamour by a bright tablecloth, while stools are topped with cushions for comfort and colour. There are a couple of fold-up chairs, too – a versatile choice, as they can be stored away neatly when not needed. A white metal cabinet adds a contemporary edge. It's the kind of piece you might find in a home office, but it works brilliantly here, providing handy storage space.

Shelves: The shelves in this room are used more for display than for storage. The only pieces of china and glass are white and orange so they key in with the room's scheme. Lined up they make an eye-catching display.

Floor: Pale wooden flooring is perfect for this bright, uplifting scheme and it's given a colour boost with a deep pink straw mat. Even when you pick a scheme like orange and white, it's a good idea to add in just one or two pieces in a different but complementary shade. This helps the room look more relaxed and less rigidly planned, and creates a contrast so you can appreciate the chief shades more.

CONTEMPORARY

The look: This is a smart, modern room with sleek furniture, designer china and sexy materials. The look is contemporary cool at its best.

Colour: The walls have been kept white and beige in this room, a neutral backdrop for all the warm wood and elegant white china. A cherrywood sideboard is a rich brown and looks great teamed with the paler wood of the table, chairs and floor. The scheme looks organic and warm and, while colour could easily be added with the china or tableware, it looks vastly sophisticated coupled with white and grey.

Furniture: Sideboards used to be naff, the sort of thing your granny kept her crystal in. Not any more. They've been reinvented as a stylish and ultra useful addition to a dining or living room. This one is in warm cherry wood with grey inset doors, looks great and creates heaps of storage space. The oak table and chairs have the clean lines of modern design, and the glass tabletop looks sharp and original.

China: Good-quality china will give a table added style and personality. These designer pieces have great shape and a beautiful ribbed surface. They give the table mountains more style and help create a sharp, sophisticated air.

Floor: Wooden boards are perfect in a dining room. They're hygienic – stray crumbs can be easily swept up – and stylish. Here, a similar wood to the table has been chosen for the floor to create a smooth, ultra coordinated look – very grown up.

CONTEMPORARY

The look: This white room uses flashes of colour to liven it up and give it a stylish finish. Minimal furniture ensures it feels open and airy while colourful accessories add personality and stop the paleness becoming plain.

Colour: This room has white walls and an off-white vinyl floor, creating a neutral, fresh backdrop. To stop it feeling drab or bleached out, two strips high up the wall have been masked off then painted a cornflower blue. This makes the room feel wider and less like a corridor. The same blue is picked up in the tablecloth, while cheery cushions and accessories create little points of colour around the room.

Furniture: Even the plainest of tables can be given a shot of chic with a pretty tablecloth. Using a perky polka dot cloth like this is a great budget option, getting maximum style from an inexpensive seen-better-days table. The table is turned sideways to fill the space, give a cosy feel and making it easy for family to gather round. White folding chairs keep the look light and can be stored neatly away if not needed, helping the room feel bigger still. Rather than installing expensive ceiling lights, adding a stool with a desk lamp on it means softer light for relaxed dining is the flick of a switch away.

Storage: A tall chest of drawers makes an efficient use of space and adds height, stopping the room feeling so long and narrow. A selection of retro pieces are displayed on the top of the chest of drawers while cookery books are tucked neatly on a shelf close to the table so you can sit and browse. Pretty collectors tins complete the display.

The look: This dining room has modern style all sewn up. From the eclectic mix of chairs and the gorgeous china to the dark slate flooring and the stylish upright storage, it's a room that's functional, but beautiful; carefully styled, but very laid back.

Colour: Colours are subtle and natural in this room. The walls are painted the palest grey and enriched by a slate floor that has splashes of amber blended in. The furniture is either black, white, cream or brown and the mix of accessories and china echo those shades, creating a soothing scheme with a natural feel.

Furniture: Who says you have to have matching chairs round a dining table? Here, there's a mix of seating. Two unusually shaped chairs add a sculptural feel to the table, and the contrasting colours add to their impact. They're teamed with a white chair in a classic shape and they sit beautifully around the rectangular wooden table.

Shelves: This room is spacious so there's room for a tall, chunky shelving unit that's home to beautiful vases and baskets. It adds a strong vertical line to the room, offsetting the horizontals of the table and wall shelf, and it gives the room height. The long wall shelf holds an eclectic mix of ceramics and glass and could double as a sideboard for serving food.

Accessories: There are lots of beautiful pieces in this room, giving it a strong decorative feel. China vases, bowls and dishes are all based around a muted palette of brown, white and cream to tone in with the room and give it interest and texture. A photograph of fruit adds some colour while a bay tree adds another strong vertical and some deep green foliage.

CONTEMPORARY

The look: Warm earth tones, stripped wood and toffee-coloured leather combine to give this room a light and easy feel. A simple table gets a shot of style from modern classic chairs in tubular steel and leather, while a huge window lets light pour in, making this clutter-free room feel extra tranquil.

Colour: Taken from an earthy, muted palette, the colours in here are easy to live with. They don't jump out at you, yet they subtly create the right atmosphere – relaxed, warm and light. The stripped wooden boards and door set the tone with their soft honey colour. Walls in pale sand and mushroom shades continue that warm, natural feel.

Furniture: This neat little room is fairly short on space, so furniture is kept minimal.

A table and chairs with clean lines help the space feel airy – the table's slim legs make it discreet and teaming it with stylish leather seats gives it a contemporary lift. A chimney alcove is home to a small unit, where a stereo is perched so there's music while you eat.

Flooring: Original pine floorboards have been stripped and varnished to create a warm, hardwearing floor. To liven it up and mark out the space where the table should stand, there's a colourful kilim rug, which adds a splash of pattern and more earthy colour to this peaceful room.

Window: Filmy tab-top curtains look great at this window, allowing plenty of light to pour in, even when they're partially closed. A wrought-iron pole and tie-backs are neat and stylish and match the iron chandelier.

CONTEMPORARY

The look: This open-plan house has a laid-back feel, with the rooms running into each other. The dining space is big and family friendly, with a huge table at its heart to eat, play and work at. Warm colours add to the friendly feel.

Colour: The maple units in the kitchen are clearly visible from the dining area so the walls have been painted a warm toffee colour that tones in. The carpet, which covers old floorboards, is in a lookalike shade and is laid throughout to create a feeling of space and the sense that rooms flow into each other.

Furniture: The table was made by fixing varnished MDF onto an old frame. To finish it off, hessian was used to hide the joins between the base and top. It's a huge table so there's always space to work, eat or play, without having to clear it off completely. Simple chairs in an organic shape add a contemporary touch and can be easily stacked out of the way when not needed.

Bookcase: This amazing, swirling bookcase works as much as a piece of art as it does a functional bit of furniture. There's space for books, plus room for decorative pieces and it's seriously good-looking. It suits this open-plan room, where the large wall is viewed from both near and far.

Lighting: Two low, pendant lights hang over the table, creating pools of light that are good for working or eating by. They also help zone this large space, literally highlighting the place where the table should go, and create a sense that this is the dining area, separate from the rest of the room.

The look: There's a cool, Scandinavian feel to this dining room. White furniture, limed floorboards, check curtains and minimal clutter create a bright, romantic room.

Colour: Scandinavian schemes are all about simple colour and lots of white, and this room has all that. To gently warm the white furniture and floor, the walls have been painted an off-white that has a touch of beige in it. Interest is added at the windows by curtains in a neutral check – just enough pattern and colour to stop the room feeling bleached out, but not so strong that the eye goes straight to them.

Furniture: Scandinavian furniture is generally elegant and shapely, so this table and chairs are perfect. These pieces were sold white, but just by painting furniture white you can lighten the atmosphere of a room and give it a Swedish flavour. The carved doors and drawers and the circular handles on the sideboard are classic Scandinavian details.

Window: Simple curtains in a subtle check look perfect in this window. They have been designed deliberately too long so that they crumple into a puddle at the bottom.

Accessories: Not all empty spaces need filling! In this room, the furniture and accessories have been carefully positioned so that each piece can be appreciated individually. This helps keep the space feeling light and uncluttered. Pewter plates and candlesticks add some steely sophistication while china with an understated sprig design, especially in blue and white, hits just the right Scandinavian note.

The look: This pretty dining room has more than a hint of French style thanks to the ornate chairs and feminine cushions, and when decorated with candles, crackers and colourful festive flowers, it's all set for Christmas, too.

Colour: Pale white walls and natural sisal flooring create the perfect neutral backdrop. Ornate white chairs tone in perfectly, while a deep blue tablecloth and assorted pretty cushions add colourful splashes of pink, red and green. Florals and gingham fabrics are perfect for creating a simple yet chic scheme.

Furniture: These ornate wrought-iron chairs originally lived in a French café, but look perfectly at home here. Painted pure white, wrought-iron furniture looks light and elegant, its curling lines more delicate than traditional wooden pieces. To best show off the chairs' unashamedly romantic style, the table has been covered with a totally plain cloth, so the chairs' design shines out against it. The plainness of the cloth is also a great backdrop for the assortment of china and glass, and stops the room feeling overly ornate or fussy.

Flooring: Fibres like jute, sisal or seagrass are just right in a shabby chic room, because they're neutral and natural.

Table top: Pretty pieces of old and heirloom china and lots of glass give this table real sparkle and character. Tall, tapered candles instantly create an inviting feel, while a simple floral display of ivy with pink and red roses creates a Christmassy feel. Finally, elegant cut-glass decanters bring some old-world charm to a fairly modern scheme, and beautifully catch and enhance the twinkling candlelight.

The look: This airy dining room takes its inspiration from the combination of green and pink so commonly seen in flowers. Lots of white, glass and texture-rich chairs and cushions make it feel as good as it looks.

Colour: Pink and green is one of nature's favourite pairings, so it's perfect as a room theme. When leafy and cool, green takes all the sugariness out of pink, making it easy to live with and grown up too. Plenty of white is mixed in to lighten the overall effect and stop the room from looking rigidly two tone.

Furniture: An ultra simple, inexpensive white dining table is teamed with tactile Lloyd Loom chairs to liven it up. Their woven finish is perfect for this natural themed room and cushions covered in deep pink fabric give them extra comfort and colour. A huge dresser in old white gives the room character and stops it feeling too modern. The drawers provide useful storage space and the shelves are great for showing off the gorgeous green and white china.

Window: The combination of a roller blind and deep green curtains gives lots of versatility, while adding some green to the scheme. Curtains also keep a big room like this feeling snug, while a blind can filter bright light.

Chandelier: Dining rooms are typically used at night, a place to gather for leisurely meals. It's important, therefore, to have some ambient light that can create a soft, relaxing atmosphere. Candles are perfect for that and this striking chandelier, a modern take on a traditional shape, has the advantage of looking good at any time of the day.

The look: Sensual lines, elegant colours and a touch of gold give this dining room a refined, romantic air. The curves of the carved wooden chair and the display cabinet have a touch of Scandinavian style about them, while the patterned wallpaper could be right out of a French château.

Colour: Colours are delicate and soft in this room, taken from a palette of aged and traditional shades. The table itself supplies a warm hint of blue, while the walls are treated to a delicately patterned wallpaper in duck egg and gold. A console, cabinet and chair in cream and distressed white look timeless while the odd splash of red on the china adds subtle interest.

Furniture: This table earns style plus points, both for its warm blue colour and interesting outline. The legs are shapely, so it deserves to be displayed in a large room where you can see and appreciate them. A curvy chair in white teams perfectly with this table – too much coloured furniture can look overwhelming and a blue chair here would spoil the subtlety of the scheme. The room is a good size so there's space for a cabinet that holds china and glass.

Walls: Wallpaper is enjoying a style revival at the moment and no wonder when it comes in so many fantastic patterns. This is a very traditional design, using subtle colours so it adds interest to walls without being distracting. If you want to use a bolder print, try pasting it up in an alcove or on a chimney breast to minimize its impact.

The look: There's an exotic, North-African feel to this dining room. A curvaceous metal table with a beautiful tiled top could be straight out of the kasbah, while plants, woven wicker and hints of rich orange conjure up warm, exotic Moorish nights.

Colour: A base shade of white helps to keep this room feeling fresh and light. You can weave in a theme like North-African style without having to paint dark colours everywhere and hang hookah pipes from the ceiling. Here, the idea is conveyed with hints of warm, spicy orange and deep blue. Dark metal and warm wood liven up the look more and add extra depth.

Furniture: Curling metal is key to the Moorish look and this table tops that by having a tiled surface. Bright tiles are central to the design and they're practical, too – creating a tough, heat-proof cover for a table. The stool looks suitably ethnic and is quite low, another hallmark of Moorish style.

Cupboard: This built-in cupboard has been given an exotic feel by the addition of a deep blue border and a decorative motif, which has been stencilled in rich orange. The orange knob is the finishing touch. Mesh inset in the door panels means the chunky earthenware pieces are visible through it, adding more colour to the room.

Accessories: Woven wicker baskets teamed with solid earthenware in strong blues and terracotta are simple, welcoming and unpretentious – just right for this scheme. Stand potted plants in woven containers to add a lush, natural feel. The orange rug warms up the stone floor, and adds both rich colour and kasbah cool.

The look: It's light, it's fresh, it's cool. This dining room uses pale shades and plenty of white furniture to create an airy feel and clean scene. It's a simple scheme that relies on a few key ingredients and colours, all combining to create a really fresh, romantic room.

Colour: There's plenty of white in this room but, rather originally, not on the walls. The table, chairs and shelving unit are all in clean white, as is the mirror frame. Floorboards are pale and subtle and the walls are where the soft lilac colours are introduced. Cool tones make walls appear further away and here, the soft grey and misty lilac enhance the feeling of space. A lilac tablecloth and napkins, plus the odd splash of blue and purple on glassware and china, add more soft colour.

Furniture: A white table and chairs are ideal in a room that doesn't get much light – they look so fresh. A white tabletop will create a sense of space and bounce light around. The simple lines of this furniture contrast with the contemporary boxy unit that works as storage and display space and helps to add interest to this pale room.

Mirror: A tall mirror is a really useful addition to any interior. This one is almost door size and, as it reflects the shelving unit, it gives the sense that there's another lookalike room leading off this one. Mirrors also reflect what light there is around the room, making it feel brighter and bigger.

Accessories: The shelving unit is the perfect place to show off gorgeous glass and china. Pieces are on hand when you lay the table and can be moved about to create fresh displays as often as you like.

The look: White, light and the sweetest, softest pink create a dining room that's beautifully serene and elegant. Chairs draped with ghostly white covers and delicate glassware complete the look, while a beautiful chandelier adds a touch of glamour.

Colour: Pink isn't just a colour for little girls' rooms – it can look stunning anywhere. The trick is to team it with another shade that will make it seem fresh rather than sugary. Here, white does the job perfectly. Choose pinks with touches of plum or purple in them for a sophisticated feel, then add lashings of white for a stylish, fresh scheme.

Furniture: White cotton covers have been used to give a random mix of old junk-shop chairs a stunningly elegant feel. Choose a fabric that is machine washable so the covers can be popped in the wash to refresh them. Money saved on the chairs has been invested in a handsome extending dining table – so beautiful it would be a shame to cover it with a tablecloth.

Window: Simple Roman blinds use a minimum of fabric so you can afford to splurge on a beautiful material like this elegant toile de jouy. It keeps to the white and pink theme but adds some subtle pattern to the room.

Fireplace: This handsome pale stone fire surround is a style asset, and instead of cluttering the mantelpiece with lots of pieces, a show-stopping photograph of a plant has been hung directly above. This adds plenty of interest without the fuss of lots of little accessories. The chimney breast wall behind it has been kept white to help show it off.

The look: This dining room uses a mix of textures to create a sensual room that feels as good as it looks. The colours are muted and natural, allowing the mix of natural fibres, shiny glass, sparkly china and woven rug to shine out.

Colour: Many of the materials in this dining room are natural – rush, rattan, wool, leather – so it's right that the colour scheme is natural too. A blend of soft greens, rich chocolate brown and cream combine effortlessly together, giving this room an easy-to-live-with, timeless feel.

Furniture: Textures are mixed and matched to create a visual and sensual feast. Woven rush and metal chairs, bursting with texture, are teamed with a sleek and reflective glass topped table. Meanwhile, for a touch of luxury, the console table by the wall is covered in deep brown leather, which makes an unusual but very sleek and soft surface.

Flooring: This show-stopping bubble weave rug is so thick and bobbly it almost looks like pebbles on a beach. It adds lots of welcome interest and texture to the floor and feels sensational under bare feet, too.

Accessories: Again, pieces in a range of textures have been deliberately chosen for maximum style mileage. Mugs with a silvery lustre sit on a soft, muted linen table runner. Shiny glass candle holders stand next to a matt black dish with hard, knotty rattan balls arranged in it. The silky richness of the leather console is enlivened by the shiny vase and plate and the lacquer box. This play between textures and surfaces takes a muted scheme from subtle to sensational.

The look: A mismatched set of old chairs and a chunky table get an elegant lift thanks to lengths of sari fabric that are used to make exotic cushion covers and a stunning tablecloth. Modern white china livens up the dark wood furniture for an east meets west, old meets new, look.

Colour: Pale green walls create a fresh backdrop which, blended with lots of white (on woodwork, china and curtains), looks super stylish. The gold pattern of the darker green sari fabric adds a shot of exoticism.

Furniture: Dark wood furniture is very in these days, so although these chairs are old their treacle colour has a contemporary feel. They've been waxed to cover old scratches and give them a rich sheen, and their cushions have been covered with sari fabric. There's plenty of space in this dining room, so the large dark wood sideboard has room to breathe. Quirky modern vases in sculptural shapes give a fresh slant to this traditional piece of furniture.

Fabric: Saris come in long lengths so they're ideal for using as a tablecloth. To make the cushions, two layers of wadding were covered with the sari material and then pretty gold and green ribbon was stitched to either end with Velcro to secure them to the chairs.

Lighting: Two pendant lights hang low over the table, with neat white shades that tie in well with the china and curtains. These create soft pools of light that are perfect for dining by and, when all other lights are switched off, they accentuate the table's position at the centre of the room.

The look: There's a nostalgic, Thirties feel to this elegant dining room, thanks to the shapely wooden fire surround, the paintwork and the dresser. Stripped boards and stylish chairs add a contemporary touch, bringing the scheme up to date and making it easy to live with.

Colour: A high dado rail around the room – a classic Thirties feature – divides up the walls, and different coloured paints draw attention to it. Above, the walls are white, while below a thin strip of palest green creates a pretty border around the room. Thirties interiors often features borders and lines of paintwork, which have the effect of framing a room. The green chosen here matches the green on the original dresser – a nice touch. Below is a soft cream – warm, sunny, practical.

Furniture: This original Thirties dresser, which was found in an antiques shop, looks beautiful tucked into the chimney breast alcove. Next to it, a glowing wooden fire surround in a geometric, boxy shape, which is so typical of Thirties design, adds another authentic note. Simple wooden chairs and a large, rectangular table look timeless and would fit into any room scheme. Here, their wood perfectly complements the stripped floorboards. The key to this room's success is this mixing of old and new. It stops the room feeling too 'themed' or like a museum piece, and preserves its elegant, Thirties flavour.

Accessories: In a room with a strong style identity, accessories can really help, picking up the theme without making as bold a statement as a piece of furniture can. Here, the clock on the wall and the wooden picture frame pick up the Thirties feel, but look subtle and stylish.

ELEGANT

The look: This room has a distinctive, classic charm thanks to bold black and white wallpaper and splashes of strong blue. These graphic elements are softened with white dining room furniture and a textured wool carpet in a soft oatmeal shade.

Colour: A monochrome scheme is the key component of this room. Graphic toile de chine fabric at the window and matching wallpaper look strong and are given a fresh kick with plenty of white. As if this wasn't eye-catching enough, a bright blue is painted on the panelling around the lower half of the walls. It's a bold move but it pays off, adding a quirky, contemporary feel.

Walls: This striking, toile de chine wallpaper is not for the faint hearted. It gives the room a strong, slightly old-style feel and is the first thing that catches the eye when you walk in. It's been used on all the walls and teamed with a matching blind for a really uncompromising look. If you like the style but don't want the full-on effect, try using a wallpaper like this just in an alcove or on a chimney breast.

Furniture: The table and chairs look stylish and timeless. The chairs' rounded shape and carved backs give them classic elegance, while their soft blue seat covers tie in with the blue walls. The white table has a dark wooden top to add a welcome note of warmth to the scheme. Its legs are slightly tapered at the base to give it a lighter feel.

Accessories: The vases, plant pots, china and glassware are defiantly modern, helping to bring the room up to date and balance out its traditional elements. A huge mirror breaks up the wallpaper pattern while oversized vases look sensual and modern. Pretty china and bubbly blue glasses add some fun to what might otherwise be a very grown-up look.

The look: Warm tones of yellow and green, elegant furniture and lots of light give this room lashings of grown-up style.

Colour: A dado rail running mid-height around the room creates a natural border, and different shades have been painted either side of it. Above, an egg-yolk yellow gives the room a rich, sunny feel; below, a shade of strong, blueish-green adds interest and contrast. A beautiful wooden cabinet is built into an alcove, its rich, polished wood teaming beautifully with the yellow walls, while yellow curtains and creamy seat covers add more coordinating colour.

Furniture: There's a mix of furniture here. The table, with its glass top and graphic shape, looks sharp and modern. The chairs, although new, are a classic style and are simply upholstered in hardwearing cotton twill. The cabinet looks stylish and elegant, its gleaming wood and stunning craftsmanship giving the room real elegance. Glass-topped tables are a real asset in a dining room, especially if it doesn't get much light. They look light and ethereal, stopping the room feeling blocked off as it can do with a dark wood table, and help it to feel bigger.

Curtains: Another note of timeless elegance crops up at the windows. A heavy, golden curtain pulls across to one side and adds an almost Victorian feel. Fringing along its edge and top adds a luxurious touch, while thick, tasselled tie-backs complete the effect and allow the curtain to be fixed back with a deep sweep.

Flooring: Pale wooden flooring creates a simple, neutral backdrop. It's warmed up by a large rug in a mushroom shade, which also helps delineate the dining area. Make sure rugs are large enough for all the chairs to sit comfortably on top.

ELEGANT

The look: A warm, cosy, gentleman's club was the inspiration for this traditional dining room. Dark colours, elegant furniture and a large fireplace capture the feel of a sedate smoking room from yesteryear – you can almost taste the port and cigars!

Colour: The walls have been painted a rich crimson, a warm colour that feels inviting and cosy at night when lights are low. It is perfectly complemented by the parquet flooring in a dark, highly polished wood, and the equally dark wooden table and chairs. Cream curtains add a light touch at the windows, but basically this room is about rich, elegant tones.

Furniture: The table and chairs shout classic elegance. The curved lines of the long table, the beautifully carved chairs and the dark wood combine to create a rich, traditional look. A sideboard on long legs stands by the window, adding storage space and more dark, classic furniture.

Shelves: An alcove to one side of a chimney breast makes the perfect place to put up shelves. These are thin and discreet and crowded with books, which add colour and texture to the room. You can fit shelves right up to the ceiling, as here, to make the most of available space. Just make sure you don't put your favourite tomes up there, as reaching them will be awkward.

Floor: Parquet adds a world of detail to a floor, its short blocks of wood laid in alternating directions creating more interest and movement than simple floorboards. Parquet tends to be dark and often highly polished. It's readily available today but some homes, particularly from the Twenties and Thirties, still have the original thing.

The look: This room is a lighter, airier interpretation of the classic country look. There is timber furniture designed with the open shelving and solid lines of traditional rustic pieces, but it has a modern finish. The floral prints of classic country schemes are retained but used sparingly and they're set against clear, fresh colours and plenty of plain accessories and fabrics.

Colour: A subtle, powdery blue has been painted on the walls, and the colour is picked up by various pieces of pale blue china. A white-painted floor lightens the look further and this, too, is echoed with lots of pretty white china dotted across the dresser. Warm wood stops this combination from looking plain or sterile, while a pretty tablecloth adds a subtle touch of pattern.

Furniture: Getting the country look doesn't have to involve scouring fleamarkets for battered old dressers and chipped chairs. Many stores offer up-to-date pieces in solid wood with a strong, country style. This dresser, for example, has the solidity and craftsmanship of modern furniture but also the open shelves and broad lines of traditional country pieces. The table and chair are also new but their shape is inspired by older designs.

China: Country dining tables are often set with a higgledy-piggledy mix of china and earthenware that has been picked up over the years. In a modern room, you can replicate this look by choosing bright, plain pottery in one or two colours and from lots of different ranges, so you have a variety of shapes, styles and designs. This creates an informal air, and means any broken pieces are easy to replace.

The look: This cosy, light space was originally two small rooms but it has now been knocked through to create an open-plan dining room and kitchen. It has an airy, relaxed feel and its pale colour scheme is the perfect backdrop for strong furniture and accessories.

Colour: There's a light, relaxed feel to this room thanks to the white walls and predominantly pale furniture. The large table has a white base and pale wooden top, the cupboard in the alcove is pale and the kitchen beyond is painted the same white creating a calm, coordinated look. The original fireplace adds some dark colour while wooden chairs in honey tones provide warmth.

Furniture: There's an interesting mix of furniture here. A chunky dining table and chairs with woven seats add a country note, while an old Indian food cupboard, found in a reclamation yard and treated to some TLC, now holds china. It was treated to washes of emulsion paint mixed with acrylics before being roughly sanded down for a shabby chic look.

Flooring: Original floorboards with a battered, aged look suit the informal, rustic feel of this dining room. They are also very easy to live with. Decades of feet marching over them have chipped and scuffed the varnish, so marks or scratches become part of the look.

Accessories: A few dramatic pieces do the work of countless smaller accessories and look sharper and less fussy in this compact room. Two large candlesticks with a battered, rustic look and a big black and white photo add interest and tone in with the pale scheme.

The look: Huge windows that let the light pour in and plenty of vibrant colour give this dining room a fun, invigorating feel. The old wooden shutters and panelled walls lend a rustic note, which is brought up to date with strong shades and simple styling.

Colour: Bold colours team together brilliantly in this room. There's plenty of natural light to stop them feeling oppressive, plus the wooden floor, table top and mahogany chairs add more subtle, natural colour and help anchor the scheme. Original wall panelling has been given a coat of green that's toned down by the cream shutters above. Old chairs have been treated to colourful new seat covers and a reclaimed radiator has been sand blasted and painted yellow to bring it into the twenty first century.

Furniture: A pine table is a country style classic, but here it's been given a shot of extra personality as its underside and legs have been painted bold blue. It's teamed with old mahogany chairs from a reclamation yard that have been brought up to date by re-covering the seats with colourful fabric.

Radiators: These are old cast-iron models. They were picked up at a local building site, but you can find them at salvage yards and fleamarkets. Some yards sell them fully renovated, which generally involves sandblasting them to clean them before repainting them. Good yards will also pressure test them. For this, water is pumped from the mains around the radiator. As it's at a higher pressure than the water from a central heating system, any holes or cracks will show up quickly. It's best to only buy radiators that have been tested, as cracks are hard to mend.

The look: The warm wood and long lines of the furniture give this dining room a relaxed Shaker-style elegance. Rich blue walls create a sophisticated mood for dining and simple check fabric adds a note of easy style.

Colour: The rich cherry wood of the table, chairs and storage chest is teamed with deep, cornflower blue for a strong but sophisticated look. Dining rooms were traditionally painted dark colours, giving evening candlelit meals a feeling of luxury and sensuality. This blue is a modern take on the rich reds and greens traditionally used and is picked up in the cushion covers.

Furniture: The ladder-back chairs have Shaker elegance written all over them. The cheery cushions give them a homely edge but, for out-and-out elegance and a more sophisticated feel, these can be removed. The tall storage chest in matching cherry is classic Shaker again and is both beautiful and useful. It provides enough storage space for the rest of the room to be left uncluttered.

Floor: A simple, white wooden floor will instantly brighten a room, and is an ideal partner to darkly painted walls as it stops them feeling too gloomy. White floors do show up every crumb and hair so, if you do choose one, be ready with a dustpan and brush.

Accessories: For easy elegance, a few Shaker-style pieces are dotted about. The heather sits in a Shaker wooden box, while the peg rail looks good on the wall as a feature on its own.

The look: This dining room is part of an open-plan living and dining area that has a rich, eclectic feel. It's full of fascinating old furniture and unusual finds, and its pale walls and dark wooden floor are the ideal backdrop to exhibit them.

Colour: White paint with just a hint of grey creates a stylish, grown-up background for this room. It's light and subtle – the perfect neutral canvas for the room's unusual pieces. Dark wooden furniture and floorboards add depth and drama while accessories with touches of colour – blue, cream, red – soften the overall look and make it homely.

Furniture: The fruitwood dining table has an aged, rustic feel and its simple lines look nicely unfussy. It's teamed with a Fifties leather chair that complements the other furniture in the room and just begs you to sink into it. In the alcove, a chest of drawers provides storage space while an old wooden wall cabinet with glass doors is the perfect place to show off favourite glass and china.

Accessories: The unusual candle sconce on the wall is one of a pair made from driftwood. The bleached wood matches the table and fits right in with the room's emphasis on old or recycled materials. Colourful letters stand on the chest of drawers, accompanied by pretty bowls and pots. These brighten up the dark wood and create a little pool of interest in this corner. They also offset the dramatic, but rather austere, picture of skulls, and the large plaster nose that is fixed to the wall nearby.

The look: This bright little dining room has a conservatory feel thanks to the dramatic tulip-patterned curtains and wicker chairs. A mix of old and new furniture gives it bags of character and a round dining table invites cosy, sociable meals.

Colour: A soft cream on the walls sets the sunny tone and is a country-style classic. A blue rug teams well with it and breaks up the brown and cream tones of the wall unit, chairs and storage. Splashes of red and green on the curtains add further drama, while the artwork sticks to the muted shades that are found in most of the room.

Furniture: When it comes to furniture, shape and materials are key in a country-style room. Here, a round table with a chunky pedestal looks pleasingly rustic, especially when painted a pale shade, as here. The chairs have a more contemporary shape, but their wicker bases help them feel natural and countrified. The old glass-fronted wall cabinet has plenty of personality and works as both storage and display space. Two matching tall tables in either corner make an unusual addition, but look gorgeous, providing storage space for wine bottles and dining room bits.

Window: A bold tulip-design fabric hangs at the window adding some contemporary drama to the room. While it's a strong pattern, the material's background is cream like the walls so the curtains blend in and don't dominate the room.

Walls: The wall unit looks like a work of art in itself and is a great place to show off beautiful blue and white china. It ups this room's country credentials and is balanced by framed pictures on either side in warm tones of brown and cream.

The look: The outdoors has been brought in to give this dining room a Mediterranean garden feel whatever the weather. A light, sunny colour scheme, green rustic furniture and some clever paint effects create a welcoming, colourful room inspired by life alfresco.

Colour: It's not so much the colours that are key in this room, but the paint effects that have been used that give it such personality. The walls have been painted with a base coat of cream emulsion, then an ochre glaze has been mixed up and daubed onto it using random strokes and a big, soft brush. This gives a raw, mottled effect, a bit like you might find in a Tuscan farmhouse. The chest of drawers has a distressed finish, so tones of cream and terracotta peep through, while the panelled terracotta back creates a bold contrast.

Furniture: The green wooden table and chairs add a pretty, rustic note and are small enough to leave room for a large dresser. This is actually made up of two separate pieces – a chest of drawers and an old dresser top – and is perfect for showing off a mix of vibrant china.

Flooring: This dark, shiny timber floor has been salvaged from a pub. Salvage yards often sell flooring from interesting old buildings and it usually costs a lot less than putting down new wood.

Accessories: To reinforce the rural Mediterranean feel, there's a topiary motif running through the room. A tablecloth and cushions are made up in topiary print fabric, while little trees stand on the windowsill. This lends the room extra personality without making it feel too 'themed'.

The look: There's a really fresh, summery atmosphere in this dining room thanks to yellow walls, bright white furniture and splashes of soft blue. Huge windows let in lots of light, brightening the scheme further and giving the room a year-round summer feel.

Colour: Pale yellow will brighten any room and works really well in those that don't get much sunshine or natural light. This room is bright already, so the sunny colour increases the feeling of light and airiness. Blue and white are the other chief colours here, a classic mix that's the palette of Cornishware pottery and summer skies flecked with fluffy clouds. Wooden flooring is pale, but still warm, just right for this scheme.

Furniture: Simple elegance is the key to this furniture. Ladder-back chairs have been painted white to give them a sense of lightness, while the large, rectangular table is softened with a blue cloth. A white dresser, a modern take on the traditional Welsh style, has glass doors and lots of storage space. Gingham material has been used behind the shelves to give the piece an extra shot of style and to tie in with the gingham cushions.

China: White china is a classic that won't date and it's versatile, too. You can keep adding to it from any range – so long as it's white, it will match. A few pieces of classic Cornishware continue the blue and white theme and add a cosy, country feel.

The look: Old pine furniture gets a modern twist with cornflower blue walls and a stylish display of china in this welcoming room.

Colour: Two key colours combine to create a dramatic but cosy feel. The soft browns and honey shades of the old pine dresser, and the wooden table and chairs, are teamed with the strong cornflower blue on the walls. The scheme is punctuated with fresh white on the curtains and touches of crimson, white and cream on the collection of old china.

Furniture: There are no new pieces in this room and this is what gives it its countrified charm. The old pine dresser base was stripped to reveal beautiful wood while the 1920s dining table has a deeper, varnished glow. An old church chair, complete with hymn book pocket, adds further character, while a selection of baskets create storage space and tone in with the wood perfectly.

Window: Simple, fine white curtains are hung at the window, providing a shot of freshness in this striking scheme. Along the windowsill, colourful silk anemones stand in Moroccan-style tea glasses. They add a pretty touch and, being silk, will last and last.

China: A selection of old china dotted randomly across the dresser top makes a pretty addition to this room. The spotty designs look fun, rustic and quaint – definitely not from a contemporary collection. It's easy to start a collection like this. Just pick a theme (a colour or design) and keep your eyes peeled in junk shops and markets.

The look: Classic country ingredients – the dresser, the wooden floor, the chunky table – get an original, creative twist in this unique room. The flooring has writing on it, the dresser has a finish that's deliberately designed to chip and become distressed, and a deliciously ornate wirework chandelier hangs low over the table.

Colour: The walls are a soft cream in this room so the dramatic pieces can sing out against it. The dresser is a pale aqua shade while plenty of warm, glowing wood is woven in thanks to the floor and table.

Furniture: The rustic table was put together using an old wooden restaurant sign for its top. It's brimming with character, so smart, contemporary chairs with cream covers were chosen to go with it – their simplicity is a perfect foil for the table. An old wooden dresser has been painted an aqua shade with a mix of emulsion and gouache, which has a slightly gluey consistency. The paint is slowly getting bashed and flaked off to give the piece an aged, distressed feel.

Floor: This floor is highly original. Words were written across it in charcoal and then varnish was applied to seal them in place and give the wood a soft sheen. It's an unusual look that works brilliantly in this eclectic room.

Chandelier: Lighting doesn't have to be purely functional. This ornate, wirework chandelier is incredibly beautiful, whether it's providing light or not. Candles can be sat in it for a warm, romantic evening light. It's hung low so its shape and detail can be fully appreciated.

The look: A dark room has been given year-round sunshine thanks to warm yellow walls and a simple window treatment. Unfussy wooden furniture and a colourful rug complete the relaxed feel.

Colour: A rich, egg-yolk yellow like this suits a dark room because it gives the impression of sunlight and instantly adds warmth. White glossed woodwork looks fresh alongside it, while stripped pine floorboards add a similar note of golden, warm colour. A terracotta rug breaks up the boards and adds richer, earthier tones that balance the yellow and team well with the wooden furniture.

Furniture: This simple table and chairs look neat and rustic. The table has slim legs, tapered at the bottom and the chairs are a classic shape. An oak cabinet on the wall provides a little storage space and its rich wooden tones are perfect in this room.

Shelves: An alcove is a perfect place for shelves but, instead of running them from floor to ceiling, these shelves are fitted up high. This has several advantages. The shelves still provide invaluable storage space, but they take up less room. The design also means that the alcove space is left largely unused so that the table can be tucked over towards the window with room for a chair in the recess.

Accessories: Fresh flowers are a country dining room essential. Don't worry about arranging them neatly, just pop a big bunch in a vase or, for a real country look, try displaying them in an old jug, jar or mug for a relaxed, informal look.

The look: The mood is clean and serene in this pretty, white dining room. There's plenty of natural light thanks to huge French windows, and white walls, furniture and china make the most of that, setting a relaxed, fresh tone.

Colour: A simple scheme of fresh white with flashes of red gives this room a strong, clean direction. The gingham seat cushions and white furniture have a Scandinavian feel, while delicate floral curtains add touches of soft red and green at the window without dominating the scheme.

Furniture: The table and chairs originally had a dark wood stain, but have been given a lick of white satinwood paint to brighten them. The tabletop now helps bounce light around the room, making it feel even brighter. To make the chairs more comfortable and stylish, cushion covers have been stitched from red and white gingham fabric, with gingham ribbon to secure them. This helps give these chunky chairs a more delicate, feminine feel, just right for this airy room.

Floor: Flooring can really help lighten a room. Choose something pale and it will reflect natural and artificial light up and around the room. Here, bamboo has been used, an eco-friendly, sustainable material that's tough and good looking – ideal for a room that sees lots of activity.

Window: Heavy curtains would look wrong in this room, which is light and bright. The windows are large so lots of fabric is needed to make curtains big enough to pull across them. They do, however, look out onto the private garden, so there's no need to choose a material that will keep out prying eyes. These fine curtains are ideal, as they keep the room looking light, provide just enough privacy and add a soft, pretty pattern to this mostly white scheme.

The look: This light living room is packed with clever touches and sensual pieces to make it as comfortable as it is beautiful. A mix of leather and faux suede; sparkling glass and polished stone; and woven fibres and softest cashmere create a tactile haven.

Colour: Restful colours have been used throughout for a peaceful atmosphere. Calm blue is warmed by natural tones on the walls, while a mix of soft cream cashmere, warm chestnut leather, natural fibres and wood adds richness and depth to the pale backdrop.

Furniture: A leather sofa is a contemporary classic that won't date. It's an investment buy that is not cheap, but it will last well and look better with age and use when the leather matures and softens. Choose the biggest sofa you can fit in your room so you can stretch out in comfort, then team it with an armchair in a contrasting material. A simple, modern, teak coffee table with strong, boxy lines is another useful addition that can be easily stored against a wall when not in use.

Window: Interlined curtains in tactile faux suede look rich and opulent as they pool on the floor. They also insulate the room and exclude draughts – good news, as a fifth of all heat is lost through windows. The curtains are made from two different coloured materials to create a wide border at the bottom – a nice, decorative touch on otherwise plain curtains.

Accessories: These add more sensuality and texture to the room. Shiny glass vases, a smooth wooden vessel and a cashmere throw for snuggling into in the evening create a tactile playground. Choose houseplants that are naturally scented to add a note of fragrance to the room.

CONTEMPORARY

The look: Rich, spicy colours join forces with natural elements here. A timbered floor against a neutral background, accessories in hot tones and a sweep of orange in the curtains and artwork give the whole room a rich glow.

Colour: Hot, spicy shades like orange, rich green and deep red love to take over so they work best when used as accents, rather than all over the walls. Here, walls are painted a hessian shade and teamed with a sofa in matching fabric, creating a background that's pale and neutral. Dark, warm tones are added here by a mahogany floor and console table and the really spicy shades are confined to the curtain, a border on the blind and the cushions – just enough colour to enliven the scheme, but not so much that it dominates.

Furniture: A really comfortable sofa is a must-have in any living room, and this one has deep feather-filled back and seat cushions for major snuggle appeal. If you're opting for a light-coloured fabric, make sure covers are loose and washable, so you won't be stuck with grubby marks or stains. A contemporary side table and unit on casters are versatile and flexible – wheel them to any part of the room – and look striking teamed with a more traditional dark wood console.

Window: A blind and curtains hang at this window, offering great versatility. Pull the blind down slightly for privacy or to keep out sunlight, then draw the curtains at night for extra insulation. Alternatively, you can hang curtains that are too narrow to draw right across, just to add colour, vertical lines and softness at a window.

CONTEMPORARY

The look: This room has lots of natural light and beautiful original features so a pale, modern scheme suits it perfectly. Shelves and storage keep clutter under control, leaving space for decorative extras that give the room tons of sophisticated personality.

Colour: Pale blue walls and whitewashed floorboards create a bright and modern look. An all-white scheme can look rather stark, but just adding chalky baby blue to the walls gives the space a softer, more easy-going feel. Cushions and throws add splashes of bright cerise, blue and pink, and these can be swapped around or added to any time to change the feel.

Floor: White floorboards boost the light in a room and look cool and modern. The boards have been stripped, whitewashed with emulsion, and then treated with three coats of clear floor varnish. This means they are thoroughly sealed and very hard wearing, ideal for a space that sees lots of traffic and activity.

Furniture: The pale sofa has removable, washable covers, a practical bonus that is essential in a family house full of kids with sticky fingers. Low-level seating with the floor cushion and leather pouf are again ideal for children and they give the room an instantly relaxed feel. The low coffee table provides an extra way to keep things out of sight, but close to hand. It can also be wheeled out of the way when more space is needed.

Accessories: A show stopping mirror creates a focal point over the mantelpiece, while smaller pieces – candles, photos, vases – give the shelves a pretty, as well as practical edge. A bright cerise cushion adds a shot of oriental glamour and is tamed by the woolly grey cushion next to it – a perfect mix of comfort and contemporary style.

CONTEMPORARY

The look: This room is very simply decorated with warm, natural colours, but a few clever details and inventive touches give it plenty of personality and help every corner and space work hard.

Colour: Natural colours give this room an airy, modern feel. Straw-coloured walls and an oatmeal carpet create a sunny look that's simple and coordinated. A terracotta sofa adds further warmth and nicely breaks up all the yellow tones.

Furniture: This room is all about relaxation and entertaining. Sofas and chairs are soft and inviting, a simple coffee table provides a place for cups and food when friends gather round and a tall CD rack means music is stored on hand.

Accessories: Space has been cleverly used here to squeeze the most out of this room. The dead space above the radiator has been made an asset by fitting a simple shelf above it. This makes a place for pictures and favourite vases, while its curly brackets create a place to hang lanterns, so candles can be lit in the evenings. To keep surfaces clear, a metal bracket is hung from the walls to hang a plant pot from. This means there's some green in the room, which is a lovely addition, without the need to clutter up a table or shelf. Likewise, a pair of vases sits on the floor, rather than a table, making a feature of an otherwise nondescript space and softening the appearance of the tall CD tower.

The look: A fresh, spring-like feel makes this room cheerful and bright. Big windows allow lots of natural light to flood in, while the mix of aquamarine walls, pretty floral cushions and curtains and the lilac sofa creates an inviting and invigorating atmosphere.

Colour: There's a bold mix of the latest lilac and aquamarine shades here, but the combination on the walls and sofa works well. It's picked up around the room with blue glasses and vases, lilac patterned cushions and a rug with a mix of lavender and blue shades. Filmy curtains add a light touch to this colour-rich scheme.

Sofa: This massive sofa is big enough to seat a whole family. It adds a luxurious note to the room, but its simple, clean, contemporary lines stop it from seeming oppressively big. Piling it with cushions in a mix of patterns and materials makes it feel soft and welcoming – a place to stretch out and relax. The room is also big enough to comfortably accommodate it – a crucial consideration as a small room can feel crowded out by a large sofa.

Windows: The filmy sheer voile used to make the curtains is wonderfully romantic and spring-like. It lets maximum natural light flood into the room and the floral pattern adds a really pretty, feminine edge. Sheer curtains are ideal in a room that's overlooked, as they can be drawn by day to give privacy without cutting out essential natural light.

Accessories: Sparkling glassware will always make a room feel brighter and more vibrant as it catches the light and adds sparkle. In this room, bold blue and turquoise glass pieces in the window match the walls and help to tie the room together.

The look: Pale lavender walls, a white varnished floor and a classic sofa sprinkled with sexy, modern cushions, give this room a light, inviting feel. There's room for displaying favourite glassware and candlesticks, but the space feels uncluttered and serene – just right for relaxing in after a hectic day.

Colour: A matt lavender paint on the walls maximizes this room's sense of space, while a white painted floor helps bounce light around. This backdrop is jazzed up with a palette of mocha, lime, teal and plum on cushions and glassware – a contemporary mix of shades that look stylish but soft, giving the room plenty of interest.

Furniture: A mix of classic, cutting-edge and revamped furniture gives this room lashings of personality. The new sofa has an elegant shape and neat wooden feet on casters, but to bring it up to date it's teamed with a cool contemporary armchair with sharp lines and a wooden and metal frame. An antique chair with wooden arms was simply re-covered in cream fabric to help it tie in with its modern neighbour. This mix of old and new extends to the room's other pieces. A contemporary, block coffee table and a sleek nest of tables rub shoulders with a tall, skinny, dark wooden console table that has old-style colour and good looks.

Fireplace: The original fire surround was ripped out years ago, so in its place there's a modern, limestone fireplace. Simply styled with strong lines and a boxy shape, its cool colour and tactile surface are perfect for this contemporary room. It also gets a shot of bright colour from the glasses and vases dotted along the white mantelpiece.

The look: A cool sense of order, a pared down but bold colour scheme and a touch of drama characterize this living room. Crisp, clean lines, strong shades and lots of contemporary accessories give it smart style.

Colour: Bold contrast is key to this room's colour scheme. White walls and a white sofa are teamed with strong red, slate grey and darkest brown for a crisp, uncompromising look. These colours are strictly adhered to, giving the room a very precise, defined look that's modern and urban.

Furniture: The square lines and neat geometry of the bookcase and coffee table suit this precise scheme but, in truth, the sofa, bookcase and coffee table are all classically-shaped pieces that would look just a good in a soft, pastel room as

in this city-slick scheme. It's the styling and accessories that give them their tough edge – they all get a shot of Eighties drama with red and grey cushions, throws, books and vases.

Windows: Sweeping curtains or filmy fabrics would look glaringly out of place in a pin-sharp room like this but these soft grey roller blinds are ideal – they're very stylish with a pattern that echoes the square shapes elsewhere in the room.

Accessories: This is where the really bright, dramatic colours come in. Bold red and deep grey cushions, throws and vases take this scheme from simple to stunning. The beauty of having a neutral backdrop and simple furniture is that you can reinvent it with accessories as often as you like.

The look: This contemporary room mixes modern textures with quality wooden furniture for a look that's easy to live with and long lasting. Pale walls make a peaceful backdrop, allowing a classic leather sofa and a stunning coffee table to be the main attractions.

Colour: The walls have been painted an off-white that is shot through with softest lilac for a backdrop that's neutral, but not boring. The purple note is picked up on a ruched cushion, some modern art and a sensual glass vase. Elsewhere, deep brown adds warmth and a wooden table brings glowing, natural tones.

Furniture: A dark leather sofa designed with a boxy shape brings plenty of simple, contemporary cool to this room. It's teamed with a good-quality wooden coffee table, complete with drawers and shelves for storage – a combination that looks timeless and elegant. A couple of floating shelves are the only other additions, echoing the clean lines and no-fuss feel of the other pieces.

Fireplace: Where a fancy Victorian fireplace once stood, there is now a simple, modern, hole-in-the-wall design. The mantelpiece has been removed and the area plastered smooth. This creates an ideal nook for displaying beautiful pieces. Candles can be lit for a mock-fire feel at night, while a wooden shoe last and some sexy modern vases blend old and new perfectly.

Accessories: These soften the room, adding tactile texture and colour. A woven blanket with mountains of feel appeal and a ruched cushion break up the neat lines of the sofa and invite you to snuggle down. Glass vases and bowls reflect the light, their sleek shapes adding another contemporary touch, while books and papers give the room a lived-in, welcoming feel.

CONTEMPORARY

The look: There's an organic look to this living room. Like nature, it's all about contrasts – natural textiles in wool, wicker and leather blend with simple woods, while green accents freshen up a colour scheme of mineral hues.

Colour: A slatey grey creates a subtle backdrop and sets the natural, pale tone of the whole room. Added to this are a white wool carpet, a cream sofa and plenty of solid, warm wood. A dark leather chair adds warm chestnut tones, while houseplants add freshness and greenery.

Furniture: All the pieces in this room have either rustic textures, like the wicker lounger; welcoming softness, like the sofa and leather armchair; or a reassuring natural chunkiness, like the simple solid oak table and the sideboard. They combine to create a natural, organic room that feels and looks gorgeous.

Flooring: Choosing a carpet with maximum feel appeal is a great way to weave more luxurious texture into the room. This thickly woven wool carpet plays on the room's tactile theme, adding subtle detail to the neutral scheme. Unlike some natural fibres, like sisal or seagrass, it's also incredibly soft underfoot.

Accessories: To pull the room together, accessories with natural motifs and organic shapes are dotted around. Pieces of stylish ceramic pottery with soft shapes look great against the oak table, while tiles with a dandelion pattern add a natural note to the walls. Candles in the fireplace provide soft light in the evenings while houseplants add a shot of lush green straight from nature.

The look: Pale yellow is teamed with white and cream for a fresh but easy-to-live-with look. Plenty of natural materials and weathered wood give it warmth while a tall chest of drawers ensures clutter is kept under control.

Colour: Stimulating yellow is good for rooms where you socialize and is an instant space reviver, but it loves to be loud. The trick to using it is to pick the palest of yellows, tone it down with some creams and whites, and then add a little warmth with a biscuit-coloured rug, floral and stripey cushions and curtains in tactile, oatmeal linen.

Furniture: Natural materials feature heavily in this room, helping to anchor the zingy yellow. A woven armchair adds mountains of texture and a slightly colonial feel, while a low wooden bench table in stunning wood adds warmth

and is ideal for kids to use. The creamy sofa has a simple, classic shape and lightens the room, while a tall chest of drawers is perfectly placed in an alcove, adding interest and loads of storage space.

Flooring: The floorboards are pale and weathered, with a beach-bleached look, just right for keeping this room feeling light. They're given some texture with a biscuit-coloured sisal rug. A natural fibre, sisal is hard wearing and tough, ideal for a room where kids will be running about.

Fireplace: This hole-in-the-wall fireplace is filled with beautiful pieces. A mirror makes it look twice as big, while flowers and books give it a nice relaxed feel. Above, in the absence of a mantelpiece, a floating picture shelf has been hung and is home to a random collection of pieces which create a pretty effect.

The look: Strong red walls and curtains give this room a heart-warming feel whatever the weather. Dark timber accents, rich textiles and reflective glassware and accessories combine for a look that's grown up and fiery.

Colour: Red boosts your spirits and sense of warmth, making a strong, rich statement. Here, the bold red of the walls and curtains is balanced by crisp white woodwork, understated cream flooring and lots of smooth, light-reflecting surfaces. Richer accents of brown are woven in with the sofa and wooden furniture, adding a soothing, natural note that takes the vibrant edge off all that red.

Furniture: Everything shouts classic in this living room. A soft sofa in a traditional shape sits comfortably with a wooden coffee table and sideboard, both providing useful storage space and both so elegant that they won't go out of fashion. A scattering of cushions gives the sofa colour and stops it looking bland, while a leather footstool adds another dose of bright-as-you-like red.

Fireplace: This fireplace, with its classically-shaped marble surround, makes an elegant centrepiece. A Venetian mirror above adds more classic style points, but propping it on the mantelpiece rather than hanging it gives it a nice informal edge. A selection of dramatic vases in red or dark timber add modern drama and continue the key colour themes.

Lighting: Ornate chandeliers have been used to light homes for hundreds of years, but this design has stunning red glass droplets for a classic meets contemporary feel. The droplets also catch the light from the window or the bulbs and reflect it around the room.

The look: The Thirties are the inspiration for this living room. Modern essentials, such as a TV and video, rub shoulders with the Thirties-style fireplace and furniture. A striking border design has been painted around the walls.

Colour: Creamy walls give a light, sunny feel to this room. The unit that houses the TV and video cassettes has also been painted cream, and plain cream curtains hang at the windows. A very Thirties touch of colour has been added by a thick border of red and dark green paint that runs around the walls and skirting board, framing the room and lifting the cream colour scheme.

Fireplace: This fire surround was built following an original Thirties design. It has a strongly geometric feel with a taller piece of wood inset in the centre directly over the fire-place. The wood also extends to make a border for the hearth and matches the floorboards

beautifully. The rest of the fireplace is tiled in fresh white and once more a geometric line pattern is incorporated. A thick border of black tiles frames the cast iron fire pit, adding plenty of definition.

Furniture: The unit beside the fireplace was designed especially for this room so it fits the space exactly and provides plenty of storage for the TV, video and tapes. Rather than being just a simple rectangular shape it has a rounded edge that makes it fit beautifully into the corner. Rounded corners were modern and innovative in the Thirties and were incorporated in many houses of the period.

Accessories: This room is neat and clutter free but, to reinforce the Thirties theme, there are two old photos in Deco-style frames on the mantelpiece. The round mirror above, hanging from the picture rail, completes the look.

CLASSIC

The look: The delicious colours of chocolate, from creamy milk to the darkest, bitterest cocoa, give this room a rich, exotic feel. Teamed with soft white it looks bold and strong, while accents of deep purple pep up the scheme.

Colour: If you go for creamy white on most of the walls you can afford to be brave and add lots of rich, chocolatey tones elsewhere. Here, a deep brown carpet, cushions in a mix of cocoa shades and lavish silk curtains create a sophisticated feel. Shots of purple are also woven in to lift the brown and cream – think of a bar of Dairy Milk, the chocolate peeping out from its purple foil wrapper, and you have your scheme.

Furniture: From the pale sofa with deep cushions and big, rounded arms, to the neat coffee table in dark chocolate wood, the pieces in this room are simply styled and classic. Cushions lift the cool coloured sofa and add even more comfort, while a brown suede cube works as both a foot rest and stool and can be moved around the room as needed.

Windows: Lavish silk dupion fabric in a rich, chocolate shade has been used to make loose curtains. Silk needn't look stuffy. Choose a rich shade and make the curtains using generous lengths of fabric and you'll create a luxurious feel.

Cushions: Cushions are a great way to bring a mix of colours into a room and, once you tire of a pattern or shade, simply swap the cover. Here, a mix of materials have been blended together adding interesting texture contrasts, too – there's silk, suede and simple cotton for a colourful, tactile mix.

The look: Soft shades of peony pink, cream and white create a look of easy elegance. The emphasis is on relaxation in this room, and a carpet that's sinfully soft, a sink-into sofa and mountains of cushions offer unbeatable comfort.

Colour: The walls have been painted a soft, floral pink to create a feminine feel. To stop pink from feeling too sugary, team it with plenty of fresh white, which brightens and lifts. Here, cream is used to add to the relaxed atmosphere and the cushions introduce different layers of pink, from deep cerise to sugared almond.

Furniture: It's big, it's padded and it's very comfortable. The furniture in this room was built for relaxing and both the sofa and armchair are designed with deep cushions and generous curving arms for maximum squidgeyness. The room is large so the pieces don't need to be pushed up against walls and are arranged informally for an even more relaxing feel. A large footstool has a padded top so it creates comfy extra seating and the lid lifts to reveal useful storage space inside, which helps to keep the room clutter free.

Flooring: Carpet is enjoying a revival, and no wonder when there are so many fantastic varieties to choose from. This is a stylish rework of a Seventies classic – the shag-pile carpet – but forget Abigail's Party, this one is luxurious, subtly coloured and pleasingly tousled for a texture-rich, super-soft effect.

Lighting: Chandeliers are big style news these days. They suit larger rooms, where their fanciness won't dominate, and many high street stores now sell them. Extra lighting is added with a rope of pretty flower lights suspended from the curtain pole. They create ambient light that adds a warm glow and look lovely even when they're not turned on.

CLASSIC

The look: Stripped timber flooring, warm woods, handwoven rugs, artefacts from overseas and comfy chairs create a welcoming room where interesting textures rather than flamboyant patterns take pride of place.

Colour: Warm, lively colours give this room lots of character. Aubergines, olive greens, oatmeal tones and glowing wood combine to make a room that's inviting and not overly coordinated. Soft green walls go with cream curtains, which in turn go with an aubergine sofa and a rust-coloured leather armchair. The tribal artefacts bring dark notes, while the wooden floor, fireplace and console create a rich glow.

Furniture: This sofa has striking high arms for a contemporary feel, but its warm purple colour and soft velvet up its comfort quotient and stop it from looking too modern. The leather armchair shouts comfort and its soft shape and stud finish make it an old-style classic. A console table ties in with the stripped floorboards and provides space to show off favourite pieces that add to the room's personality – old suitcases, a Buddha carving, a metal bowl.

Window: A combination of beech venetian blinds and silk curtains give the windows plenty of style. The curtains soften the windows' straight lines and add to the room's laid-back, comfortable feel. The blinds allow you to control the amount of light in the room and add a slightly colonial feel, in keeping with the pieces from India that are dotted around.

Accessories: Many of these have an Indian or Far-Eastern flavour. Each piece works in isolation and as part of the room, which means there's lots to look at and enjoy here. They also create a pleasingly timeless feel where up-to-the-minute materials and patterns have no place.

The look: Although it opens onto a kitchen/diner, this living room has its own clear sense of identity. Yellows, oranges and reds give it a warm and cosy atmsophere, distinct from the other room which is lighter and paler.

Colour: A glowing, custard yellow on the walls has only been taken up to the dado rail. Above, the walls have been painted white. This helps the room feel lighter, while the dividing line makes it feel bigger, too – horizontal lines always make a space feel larger. The warmth of the yellow is built on with a rich terracotta and blue rug, wooden floorboards and plenty of cheery cushions.

Furniture: A couple of simple, comfy sofas create a relaxed atmosphere, providing plenty of seating for all the family. The largest sofa is also positioned with its back to the kitchen, so anyone sitting on it looks into the living room and isn't distracted by the room behind and its very different feel.

Flooring: There's been a huge trend for stripping and varnishing old floorboards in the last decade, but they can be hard underfoot. To soften their feel and appearance, a big rug with a classic pattern is spread over the floor. Rugs are far easier to clean than carpet – just take them outside and give them a good beating – and generally cost less than having wall-to-wall carpet fitted.

Accessories: Colourful cushions draw the eye and make the soft sofa even more inviting. Artwork is kept to a minimum to let the yellow sing out, but a mobile of tropical fish adds a fun note in one corner – perfect for gazing up at when you're lying on the sofa.

The look: It's not the most obvious of colour combinations, but here the balance of lilac and bright red works brilliantly. Knobbly fabrics and woolly accessories add texture, while a large, striking fireplace gives the room grand style.

Colour: Soft lilac on the walls is teamed with a richer lavender shade on the sofa and carpet. Dark wooden furniture adds a classic, stylish feel to this powdery wall colour, while flashes of red create a bright contrast that, used in small doses, gives the room energy.

Furniture: Some stock living-room furniture faithfuls look great here. A comfy, rounded sofa, a simple, dark wooden coffee table and a neat console in an alcove (the ideal place for a lamp and a few favourite treasures) add up to a classic combination. They make the room feel stylish, but homely; comfortable, but also practical.

Fireplace: This fireplace is a whopper, with a carved marble surround, metal fire basket and even a metal border around that. It's extremely handsome and dictates the rather classic feel of this room. Its long mantelpiece is home to a mix of paintings and a stylish vase or two with simple lines and plain colours. Lots of small pieces would look lost and busy up here.

Accessories: There's an unfussy, elegant feel to this room and the accessories reflect that. Strong shapes work best, and large pieces like the bowl and chest on the console table make a clean, clear impact that's just right in this simple, striking room.

The look: This small living room has a modern country feel thanks to lots of stripped wood and touches of soft lilac and purple. A large fireplace makes a focal point in the room, filled with candles and pebbles for a rustic feel, while an old dresser provides room for storage and display.

Colour: Walls are a fresh, clean white, but don't look stark because they're warmed up by all the wood. Stripped doors, floorboards and a chunky old dresser bring mellow colour to the scheme, while touches of purple give the room a pretty lift. Painting the back of the fireplace a soft lilac has helped make more of a feature of the fireplace.

Fireplace: Chunks of railway sleeper make a good stage for the church candles, which flicker beautifully at night and create a relaxing atmosphere. Pebbles and driftwood scattered over the sleepers add a seasidey feel, while a large wire basket provides storage space for newspapers, helping to keep the room tidy.

Furniture: Who says dressers belong in a kitchen? A characterful old piece like this looks great anywhere. It's the essence of country style, but also brings invaluable storage space to the room – if you have kids, it's great for stashing toys in at the end of the day. Its shelves are left fairly uncluttered so the warm wood shines out, but a jug of sweet peas adds a pretty, country note. A small folding table provides a place to perch a cup while sitting on the sofa, but it can be folded away when extra space is needed.

The look: A mix of vibrant colours, characterful old furniture and original features that have been loved back to life, together with some interesting accessories and artwork, creates a welcoming, interesting room.

Colour: The walls have been painted a vibrant Mediterranean yellow. It's a strong colour, but it's calmed down a little with an understated oatmeal carpet and rug, a dark metal fire surround and lots of old wood with a mellow feel. Curtains made from a muted lavender-coloured fabric make an unlikely partner to the yellow walls, but it works well, again cooling and softening their brightness.

Furniture: Lots of old pieces give this room easy-going country style. A large wooden trunk with striking black metal hinges and locks, creates lots of storage space, as does an old built-in pine cupboard that has been stripped and waxed to bring up its soft colour. The Lloyd Loom chair is a Thirties original, snapped up in an antiques store, and the log basket next to it echoes its woven, textured look.

Fireplace: This original cast-iron fireplace needed work to look as good as it does. It was stripped to reveal the lustrous metal, then blue tiles were fitted either side. The hearth is laid with large slate tiles that match the surround and there's space to keep a basket of logs conveniently to hand.

Accessories: Bits and bobs from around the world add to the quirky feel of this room. The colourful painting came from India, while the metal jug and leather flask are fleamarket finds. Plenty of candles mean soft lighting in the evenings is just a lighted match away.

COUNTRY

The look: This room has the shabby-chic country look all sewn up. It's filled with easy-on-the-eye pieces that are brimming with character, from junk shop treasures to grandma's hand-me-downs.

Colour: Soft, faded colours are key to this look's success. A muted violet on the walls looks dreamy and gentle, floral fabrics in bleached-out colours create pools of subtle interest, while lots of white – on the sofa, floorboards, and the fire surround – adds simplicity and freshness.

Furniture: Country schemes cry out for comfy, homely pieces with soft lines and soft materials. This squidgy sofa is perfect piled up with cushions in pretty floral fabrics. The leather armchair is another country classic – the more beaten up and worn, the better.

Walls: Wooden panelling creates an instant country feel. Use it all over, confine it to one or two sides, or run it around walls at half height. It can be used to hide a multitude of sins – rough plaster or grotty wallpaper – and looks countrified and elegant painted any shade, so long as it's soft.

Accessories: More is more in a country scheme, so forget minimalism and crowd mantelpieces and tables with pretty pieces. Country schemes find new tasks for old favourites, too – a Kilner jar becomes a vase, a teapot becomes a plant pot holder, and worn leather suitcases become a coffee table. Just mix and match for maximum impact.

The look: Fresh blue and mauve join forces together with lashings of white to create a pretty country look that's inspired by nature.

Colour: Look no further than nature for colours that make your heart sing and instantly refresh any room. Fresh blue on the walls combines with a warm mauve sofa and a pretty armchair covered in a large gingham check fabric in blue and white. A pale, neutral carpet, white furniture and curtains with leafy motifs combine to create a breezy, feel-good room.

Furniture: The sofa, with its relaxed shape, soft lines and simple styling, is this room's one nod to modern style. It's teamed with a neat armchair with country-feel wooden legs and a pretty check cover. The coffee table and chest of drawers share the same mix of pale good looks – a country classic – and pretty details. The table has a woven shelf and nice, turned legs, while the chest has glass inset drawers and rounded brass handles, bursting with old-style elegance.

Window: These unusual curtains are made by stitching together lengths of different coloured fabrics, for a relaxed, pretty look. Shades of green and white feature, as does a pretty blue flower-sprig design. All the fabrics are of the same weight, to give an even effect, and the curtains are simply tied at the top to wooden rings, a pretty detail that also means they're less complicated to make than tab tops.

Accessories: Fresh flowers are a country living room essential and look great in an old jar rather than a vase (reinventing uses for vessels is a great way to add country style). There is also a mix of modern and traditional pieces which gives the room a relaxed, up-to-date country look.

The look: This room layers shades of cream with ornate furniture for a sophisticated, country look. The atmosphere is serene and peaceful, with decorative touches and beautiful accessories adding an air of timeless elegance.

Colour: This room is a dream in cream – from the walls to the furniture to the flowers in a jug. A mix of finishes adds variety. The Lloyd Loom chair, the carved wooden cupboard and the slightly distressed table break up the colour and give the eye something to settle on. A touch of faded gilt on the picture frame and burnished silver on the decorative wood carving add depth, while the books and logs bring dashes of darker colour.

Furniture: The sofa is simple and discreet to allow the more decorative pieces to show off. A Lloyd Loom chair brings some texture while an ornate cupboard, its door panel removed and replaced with chicken wire, looks really elegant. A low table is a practical addition, it's a place to put cups when relaxing and it has two drawers to help keep the room clutter free.

Fireplace: This simple fireplace with its plain surround is a blank canvas for a dramatic display. An old picture frame looks gorgeous standing on it – no need for a picture inside, the frame is beautiful enough on its own. An unusual carving, perhaps once part of a larger piece of furniture, is stunning and echoes the curves of the cupboard and frame. Logs piled high add a rustic note and some welcome woody colour.

Accessories: Most of the accessories stick strongly to the cream scheme, but one or two metallic pieces have been added to pick up the light. Using metallic pieces is a good way to weave variety into a mono-colour room. They won't jar like coloured pieces, but they do break up the one-shade monotony.

The look: Space may be short, but that doesn't stop this room from being packed with comfy furniture and pretty pieces that give it oceans of charm and character. Natural, woven materials team with plain white armchairs, while pretty curtains and colourful paintwork add an airy, feminine feel.

Colour: Pastels are perfect in this room. The walls have been painted a pale green shade, while the bookcase and fire surround are a more minty-green colour. Furniture is either cream or the soft honey colour of natural fibres, but the curtains and cushions add lots of refreshing pastel colours.

Furniture: A mix of cream covered armchairs and wicker furniture fills this room for a relaxed, country feel. Even the TV stands on an old wicker hamper, while a nook under the stairs is just big enough for a basket to hold newspapers and a distressed chest of drawers with a blue/grey finish.

Fireplace: This repro fireplace was given a coat of white paint to brighten it up and help it fit in with the breezy scheme. A new wooden fire surround was added and painted in the same minty green as the bookcase. This provides space for a random selection of cards and photos that add colour, while a large mirror above helps the room feel bigger.

Flooring: An inexpensive wood laminate flooring is laid here, instantly neatening up the room and creating a hard-wearing, neutral background. Its wood effect suits a country scheme, and is also hygienic and easy to clean – just get out your dustpan and brush.

The look: There's a relaxed, sunny look to this easy-going living room. A simple backdrop of neutral walls and natural light is brightened with a cheery rug, a warm yellow sofa and some colourful artwork.

Colour: Walls have been kept plain and pale – huge windows let the sun stream in so colour isn't needed to boost brightness. The warm honey tones of wood give the room a rustic, natural feel, while yellow and blue sofas team with a cheery rug to add classic colour.

Furniture: There's nothing pretentious in this room, which is why it feels so comfortable and welcoming. Two sofas create plenty of space for relaxing, and are covered in simple, strong colours. Other pieces are equally unfussy: the coffee table is neat and slim; the chair has a country elegance, thanks to its curving lines and woven seat; a built-in unit provides discreet storage for a video; and there are baskets for bits and bobs. There's an uncluttered feel; the sunny lightness of the room is its key attraction.

Artwork: A few well-chosen pieces of colourful artwork can lift the tone of a room. Here, the neutral walls and unfussy furniture create a perfect backdrop for the two colourful posters. The frames match the other woodwork, which helps them tie in, while the art itself brings vibrant shots of red, yellow and green. Try moving pictures around or swapping them when you tire of them – it's easy to do and quickly changes a room's feel.

Flooring: In a neutral room with stripped boards, a rug is a great way to add colour and warmth. Because it's low down, bright patterns and strong colours don't leap out in the same way as painted walls, so you can afford to be bold.

The look: This living room is inspired by the rich spicy colours, low-level furniture, sumptuous rugs and swirling wrought-iron work of a North-African home.

Colour: North-African colours are rich, earthy and spicy – never garish, always mellow and sensual. Burnt oranges and golden yellows, dark reds and slatey blues all sit side by side for a room that's warm and exotic.

Furniture: Low-level seating is a key ingredient of a Moorish room, ideal for relaxed lounging. Choose stools and poufs in leather or natural woven fibres and scatter over plenty of colourful cushions with kelim or silk fabric covers. Spread multi-coloured rugs across the floor, overlapping for a random, relaxed feel that tempts you to spread out.

Walls: Borders, patterns and pretty flower motifs give these walls masses of Moorish interest. A base coat of a burnt saffron colour, washed over walls with a big brush for a slightly uneven finish, is adorned with a graphic flower pattern and a border of black, terracotta and blue. A fretwork pattern that's pure North-African style is stencilled below, for a look that's atmospheric, but subtle.

Accessories: A wrought-iron screen serves no practical purpose but brings lots of personality and pattern to the room. Lanterns add soft candlelight while tea glasses and sculptural flowers complete the look.

The look: An innovative mix of berry shades and aqua blues have been blended to give this living room lots of colour and life. Sheer muslin curtains in a deep aqua diffuse a glow of colour into the room. The walls have been painted with blocks and strips of colour, too, to create mini works of art, while accessories have been kept to a minimum to let the wall treatment sing out.

Colour: Bright fruity tones – plum, grape and redcurrant – mix with bright blues and soft charcoals for a colour-rich scheme. A deep grey carpet anchors the scheme and gives it some warmth, and colours get fresher and brighter as the eye travels up the room, giving it a sense of height.

Walls: Bold blocks of turquoise have been painted onto the upper walls, creating a dramatic effect – they look like giant works of art. Below, white and softer blue freshens the look, and a thin stripe of pink runs around the room at mid height, creating a modern, dado rail effect. It also helps make the room feel bigger, as horizontal lines draw the eye around it and stretch it out.

Furniture: Furniture is kept simple, sleek and comfortable, so there's no risk of it competing with the walls for attention. A classic leather armchair and comfy grey sofa both get a shot of brightness from round cushions in a mix of zingy colours. A simple white coffee and console table keep the room feeling fresh.

Accessories: Glassware in gorgeous purple and aqua hues fits in perfectly with this scheme, adding a light feel. Some pretty artwork is made by framing wrapping paper with a bubble pattern in similar shades, and it's propped casually on the console table, so it adds to, rather than fights with, the bright walls.

The look: Warm harvest shades match the wooden floor in this room and emphasise its sunny feel. A large collection of china and stuffed teddy bears gives it a quirky, homely feel, while reinstated original features are reminders of the house's Victorian heritage.

Colour: A sunny yellow on some walls and a Regency red on the others creates a warm, dramatic feel. Red is a strong, dominant shade, so teaming it with a softer colour is a great way to rein it in a little. Stripped and varnished boards, red tiles and a large pine chest of drawers further boost the autumnal tones, while a creamy yellow suite and a white-painted pine unit add lighter, sunnier shades.

Furniture: Lots of traditional pieces give this room a welcoming, unpretentious feel. The fireplace alcoves are big enough to fit two sizeable pieces – a chest of drawers with lots of storage space and a tall dresser with stylish lattice doors. The rest of the room is given over to comfort, with squidgy, sink-into furniture the main attraction.

Fireplace: An old gas fire was replaced with this original cast-iron Victorian surround. The raised hearth is tiled with warm red tiles, that tie in seamlessly with the red walls. Rosebud 'trees' look elegant either side.

Accessories: This room is home to a collection of bears, but they're woven in amid more familiar living room ingredients such as candles and pretty artwork. This shows how a very personal collection can fit in with a very grown-up scheme.

The look: White walls team with black and blue tones, elegant furniture in wood and metal, and patterned tiles for a look that's inspired by North-African style.

Colour: This scheme is fresh and dramatic, taking a backdrop of white and mixing in dark metal furniture and touches of cobalt blue on cushions and tiles. The carpet has a slightly speckled effect, so it's more practical (it will hide dirt better) and adds some variety to the whiteness, while a carved screen adds texture and shape.

Furniture: A soft white sofa with boxy lines is a comfortable classic that fits into any scheme. Here, it's teamed with a curling metalwork table and chaise with a Moorish feel. A contemporary lamp in the same dark metal goes well without looking fussy and a cushion with a swirling pattern is the perfect partner for the chaise, softening it while sticking to the room's colour scheme and theme.

Fireplace: This simple fireplace gets a Moorish feel with beautiful blue and white tiles laid in its hearth. These add subtle colour and pattern to the room, without interfering with the old bricks and open shape of the fireplace. This is important. For a themed room to be successful, it needs to work with the room's original features, not ride roughshod over them.

Accessories: A metal lantern, blue bowls and pretty plate all have a Moorish feel, but the remaining accessories are more contemporary. They all fit in with the white, blue and black theme for a look that hangs together effortlessly. The screen by the window adds the biggest splash of Moorish style, but it's painted white to keep it looking light and subtle. It can be easily moved around to alter the room's feel.

The look: A mix of finds from far flung travels live happily together in this spacious room, bringing back memories of overseas trips and adding a touch of Far-Eastern exoticism to a suburban living room.

Colour: The walls have been painted a soft cream, creating a clean backdrop for all the exotic furniture, while the ceiling has been painted a rich golden yellow to add a hint of sunshine without dominating the room. A chunky cream rug complements the deep browns and reds which add warmth. The curtains tie in well with the ceiling colour and help the room hang together beautifully.

Furniture: A contemporary leather sofa teams well with the Indonesian coffee table and dark wood chest of drawers. An old chair with a red velvet patterned cover fits in fine too – old, new and exotic live happily side by side here.

Lighting: To create atmospheric light in the evening, two nets of tiny bulbs have been hung in the alcoves either side of the fireplace. When on, they look like little stars and create a warm glow that's perfect for relaxing.

Window: Instead of conventional curtains, exotic sarongs from Indonesia have been hung at the windows. This is easy to do. Just buy a simple wire rail and set of curtain clips, that are strung on the wire then used to tightly grip the fabric to hang it.

The look: What would have been a simple, traditional hallway in a Victorian house has been given a hip hotel feel with aluminium stair risers, lights fitted on steps and glass bricks in the wall.

Colour: A simple scheme of cream walls and lots of stripped wood give this hallway a light, welcoming feel. The blue glass bricks, set into the far wall, cast a colourful glow into the room, bringing in natural light from the rooms beyond and waking up the classic cream scheme.

Staircase: The original wooden stair risers were too rotten and damaged to be repaired, so instead, shiny brushed-aluminium ones were fitted in their place. This gives the staircase a fantastically up-to-date look – with the new metal and the old wood mixing beautifully together. Old rotten spindles were also replaced to make the hand rail secure.

Lighting: Natural light from the back of the house makes its way into the hallway thanks to glass bricks fitted at the end. These also draw your eye along the corridor and into the main part of the house, helping to lead you in. To guide your way when walking upstairs, there are uplighters fitted in some of the stair treads. They create a wash of light up the wall, which looks warm and attractive.

Accessories: In a confined room like a hallway, artwork on walls can make the space feel even more enclosed. Here, walls are kept bare, with the lighting creating the interest without cluttering. A simple metal and glass table has space for wine bottles and a dramatic vase of flowers, creating a beautiful impression the minute you walk through the door.

The look: This spacious hallway has been given a light, airy feel with blue paints and a pale wooden floor. A magazine rack keeps papers and post tidy, while a radiator gets a slick new look with a smart wooden cover.

Colour: The same shade of blue has been used on the lower walls, beneath the dado rail, and on the door – an emulsion for walls, a tougher, eggshell paint for the woodwork. Above, there's a pale, airy blue, which makes the room feel light and spacious. A subtle leaf design has been stencilled on in green at random – an easy way to breath life into plain walls, with a pattern that's not as bold or rigidly repeated as wallpaper.

Floor: The floorboards were stripped of old, peeling varnish and lightly sanded. A ready-tinted varnish, that gives the impression of whitewash, was then painted over the boards. In a hallway, a space that sees lots of traffic, it's a good idea to choose a quick drying varnish, so the floor isn't out of bounds for too long at a time. On the stairs, carpet has been laid, which helps deaden noise when people walk up and down.

Accessories: Although this hallway is spacious, it's still been left deliberately uncluttered. A small, decorative chair by the door is a good place to plonk bags when you come in, while a wall-mounted magazine rack makes a home for post and papers. The radiator cover also provides a shelf for keys or a welcoming vase of flowers, while a pretty mirror adds to the room's light feel.

The look: Stained glass in and above the front door looks decorative and colourful, while a fresh green on walls and a smart radiator cover keeps this narrow hall looking light and neat.

Colour: A pale green paint on the walls is a spirit-lifting, welcoming shade that makes you feel good about the house from the second you step inside. A dark grey carpet will hide marks from countless feet wandering in and out, while coloured glass gives this room both light and vibrancy.

Radiator: Instead of squeezing a table into a narrow hallway, fit a shelf. It takes up less space and is a handy spot for putting down mail and keys. Here, the shelf is the top of a radiator cover made from perforated MDF. This looks attractive, hiding the radiator and giving the hallway bags of style that sets the tone for the whole house.

Walls: A large mirror hangs above the radiator and this is a great way to make a narrow hallway feel lighter and bigger. It's also the last place to check your hair before you dash out the door. A peg rail is hung near the door for coats, so they're always to hand. Try to keep only in-season coats on it so the hallway feels as uncluttered as possible.

Door: A panel of stained glass in the door and above it turns an ordinary hall into something dramatic and stunning. It vastly increases the amount of light in the room, which means rooms opening off it will also benefit, and sends coloured patterns across the floor and walls when the sun shines through it.

The look: This hallway has the feel of an old country residence, thanks to its spacious dimensions, herringbone flooring and broad staircase. Clever paint effects help give it bags of character and a rustic, aged appearance.

Colour: Colours are warm, faded and lived-in. A rich brown carpet runs up the stairs, while the floor is maple wood that brings soft, honey tones to the room. Walls have been treated with a thick wash of dark paint over a soft cream. It's then been almost rubbed away, to create an aged effect and make the plasterwork look raw and nicely textured.

Walls: Distressed paintwork creates an instantly aged effect on the walls, with its mottled quality breaking up the big expanse of wall and providing plenty of decoration. To add to this, a striking head has been painted directly onto the far wall, to look like an original fresco.

Accessories: The artistic walls, warm wooden floor and tall, wide dimensions are the key assets of this hall – accessories are not needed. The only extra is a full length coat rail, that provides lots of storage. You can make a rail like this by painting a length of wood with gloss or satinwood paint, screwing hooks to it then fixing the whole thing to the wall.

Floor: This warm, maple floor was reclaimed from an old printing works and looked black before it was sanded. Buying salvaged flooring is relatively inexpensive and a great way to pick up something with real character. Sanding can work wonders on most solid wood floors, so don't be put off by a dirty surface.

The look: This open-plan house has a hallway that leads straight onto a living space, with the stairs running up one side. Clever storage has been packed into the space making it both practical and attractive, while a wall of artwork gives the space a fresh, contemporary look.

Colour: Walls have been left white throughout, so that the hall runs seamlessly into the living area. It creates a fresh backdrop for lots of beautiful botanical artwork and is nicely broken up by the understairs storage, complete with colourful books and magazines.

Furniture: This stunning set of shelves is designed to perfectly fit under the stairs, making the most of every inch of space. Its cube design means it can fit with the stairs incline, creating an interesting step design as the boxes are stacked higher. Getting shelves made like these is not cheap, but in a house that's short on space, it's a sound investment – a neat way to creatively and effectively use spaces that would otherwise be redundant.

Artwork: A collection of botanical paintings lines the hall wall, adding colour and detail. Although they appear to be hung in a random pattern, they are in fact cleverly lined up to create strong horizontal lines running from frame to frame. This ties in well with the horizontals of the understairs storage, and helps lead the eye from the door into the house.

The look: Clever storage ideas, some nifty accessories and a warm pink scheme give this room bags of style and make it super efficient, too.

Colour: Soft pink is relaxing, warm and welcoming – just right for a hallway. Here, it's teamed with a silver radiator and shiny metal accessories, taking any of its cutesyness away and giving it a contemporary flavour. Stripped wooden floorboards help anchor the scheme with their natural colour, stopping it feeling too futuristic.

Walls: Cream and pink combine for a soft look, but a plain radiator has been sprayed with silver paint to give it a touch of glitz and break up the candy shade on the walls. Hanging a mirror reflects natural light from the window in the next room into the hallway. It also creates a focal point on the blank wall and a vital check-your-appearance-before-dashing-out pit stop. Its lipped shelf provides a home for keys, so you can always easily lay your hands on them, while a letter rack in galvanised metal means essential post never litters or gets lost.

Accessories: All the accessories in this small hall earn their space by providing storage. Some galvanised stacking boxes create an imaginative phone table, which can also double up as storage for phone directories. A shiny silver shoe rack stashes shoes away and ties in with the smart metallic look, while a hatstand creates a feature in a jiffy and provides plenty of useful storage. Final simple decorative touches are the spot rugs, creating a splash of coordinating pink on the floor and some instant feel appeal.

COUNTRY

The look: Natural materials, simple colours and a beautiful bench are the raw materials of this welcoming country-feel hallway.

Colour: Neutral, off white walls are the perfect unfussy entrance to a home, especially when teamed with a rustic tiled floor that creates a warm glow underfoot. The terracotta tiles are matched with a rich oak bench and lots of baskets in texture-rich woven fibres to keep the scheme subtly colourful.

Furniture: Halls are often long and narrow, so choose furniture with a similar shape. This stylish oak bench is perfect. It's chunky enough to feel countrified, but doesn't eat into the hall's space too much. Use it to sit on when you're taking off shoes, and stash baskets below it to store post and papers.

Flooring: Terracotta floor tiles bring an instant hit of country style. They're ideal for a hallway, which sees lots of heavy traffic, as they're tough, water resistant and easy to keep clean – just wipe them down or sweep a brush over them. For a really rustic look, hunt down old terracotta tiles from salvage yards.

Accessories: Small hallways need accessories that work hard, and these all have a purpose (as well as looking great!). A rush cushion makes perching on the bench more comfortable, while baskets help to keep the space clutter free and can be neatly stored under it. The dust brush is good looking enough to be kept out, which means it's always on hand to quickly sweep up bits, and, thanks to a stylish check cover, the ironing board is even allowed to live here!

STOCKISTS:

ONE-STOP SHOPS

DEBENHAMS
Furniture (catalogue only),
lighting, window dressings and
accessories.
Tel: 020 7408 4444
www.debenhams.com

FREEMANS
Furniture, lighting, window
dressings and accessories.
Tel: 0800 900200

HABITAT
Contemporary furniture, freestanding kitchen units, contemporary lighting and accessories.
Tel: 0845 601 0740
www.habitat.co.uk

HEAL'S
Contemporary furniture, fabrics,
lighting and accessories.
Tel: 020 7636 1666
www.heals.co.uk

IKEA
Affordable flatpack furniture,
furnishings, fabrics and lighting.
Tel: 020 8208 5600
www.ikea.co.uk

JOHN LEWIS
Wide range of furniture, fabrics,
window dressings, lighting and
accessories. Carpets fitted.
Tel: 0845 604 9049
www.johnlewis.com

LAURA ASHLEY
Classic and country-style
furniture, fabrics, window
dressings, lighting and paints.
Tel: 0870 562 2116 for stockists
0800 868100 for mail order
www.lauraashley.com

MARKS & SPENCER
Classic and modern furniture,
window dressings, lighting and
a large range of cookwear and
accessories.
Tel: 08457 624624 for furniture
020 7268 1234 customer services
www.marks-and-spencer.com

NEXT HOME
Furniture, wallpaper, paints,
window dressings and lighting.
0870 243 5435 customer services
0845 600 7000 for mail order
www.next.co.uk

ALNO UK
Innovative designs featuring the latest colours and materials.
Tel: 020 8898 4781
www.alno.co.uk

B&Q
Affordable ready-to-assemble kitchens in five different designs.
Tel: 0845 222 1000
www.diy.com

CROWN IMPERIAL
High-quality fitted kitchens in a range of styles and finishes.
Tel: 01227 742424
www.crown-imperial.co.uk

FULHAM KITCHENS
Streamlined modern kitchens.
Tel: 020 7736 6458
www.fkandf.co.uk

HARVEY JONES
Traditional and Shaker-style handmade furniture, painted or ready to paint.
Tel: 0800 917 2340

HOMEBASE
Contemporary unit designs, mostly with pale wood finishes.
Tel: 0870 900 8098
www.homebase.co.uk

MFI HOMEWORKS
Wide range of affordable styles.
Tel: 0870 241 0154
www.mfi.co.uk

NOLTE
Huge choice of contemporary designs, including pale wood, coloured and frosted glass units.
Tel: 01279 868500
www.nolte-kuechen.de

PAULA ROSA
Quality kitchens in many styles.
Tel: 01903 743322

PLAIN & SIMPLE KITCHENS
Designs ranging from hand-painted wood to sleek stainless-steel door fronts.
Tel: 0161 839 8983
www.ps4kitchens.co.uk

POGGENPOHL
Cutting-edge contemporary designs in woods and laminates.
Tel: 01908 247600
www.poggenpohl.de

WICKES
Traditional and contemporary designs, many in solid woods.
Tel: 0500 300 328
www.wickes.co.uk

REPLACEMENT UNIT DOORS AND HANDLES

CLAYTON MUNROE
Period-style door handles.
Tel: 01803 762626
www.claytonmunroe.co.uk

JAMES MAYOR FURNITURE
MDF doors in 12 different
designs, supplied ready to paint.
Tel: 0121 328 1643
www.jmf.uk.net

JUST DOORS
Ready-to-paint MDF doors
made to your dimensions in a
choice of three panelled designs.
Tel: 0870 200 1010
www.justdoors.co.uk

KITCHEN MAGIC
Kitchens redesigned around
existing units.
Tel: 0121 622 6633
www.kitchen-magic.com

KNOBS & KNOCKERS
Door knobs and handles, mostly
in traditional designs.
Tel: 020 7384 2884
www.knobsandknockers.co.uk

TURNSTYLE DESIGNS
Handcrafted door knobs made
from resin, pewter and wood.
Tel: 01271 325325
www.turnstyle-designs.com

KITCHEN APPLIANCES

AGA
Traditional range cookers,
available in many colours.
Tel: 08457 125207
www.agacookshop.co.uk

ARISTON
Specialities include stainless-
steel ovens and fridge-freezers.
Tel: 0870 010 4305
www.aristonchannel.com

BOSCH
Freestanding and built-in
appliances at mid-market prices.
Tel: 01895 838743
www.robert-bosch.co.uk

BUYERS & SELLERS
Keenly priced appliances of all
types, with many brand names.
Tel: 0845 085 5585

CANDY DOMESTIC APPLIANCES
Mid-market cookers, fridges and
washing appliances.
Tel: 0151 334 2781 for built in
01685 721222 for freestanding
www.candy-domestic.co.uk

ELECTROLUX
Cooking, cooling and washing
appliances.
Tel: 0870 595 0950
www.electrolux.co.uk

HOTPOINT
Freestanding and built-in fridges, cookers and dishwashers.
Tel: 08709 060060
www.hotpoint.co.uk

MIELE
High-quality German-made appliances.
Tel: 01235 554455
www.miele.co.uk

NEFF UK
Specialists in built-in appliances, particularly cookers.
Tel: 0870 513 3090
www.neff.co.uk

SMEG UK
Smart Italian appliances, including range cookers and fridges.
Tel: 08704 424485
www.smeguk.com

WHIRLPOOL
Wide range of mid-market built-in and freestanding appliances.
Tel: 0870 600 8989
www.whirlpool.co.uk

ZANUSSI
Stylish appliances in a large range of designs.
Tel: 0870 572 7727
www.zanussi.co.uk

ARMITAGE SHANKS
Belfast-style fireclay sinks.
Tel: 0800 866966
www.armitage-shanks.co.uk

ASTRACAST SINKS
Ceramic, stainless-steel and man-made sinks in a variety of different colours and finishes.
Tel: 01924 477466
www.astracast.co.uk

BRASS & TRADITIONAL SINKS
Traditional and modern fireclay sinks; solid brass sinks and taps.
Tel: 01291 650738
www.sinks.co.uk

FRANKE
Sinks in many materials, shapes and colours.
Tel: 0161 436 6280
www.franke.co.uk

HANSGROHE
Modern chrome taps, including Philippe Starck designs.
Tel: 01372 465655
www.hansgrohe.co.uk

LEISURE CONSUMER PRODUCTS
Stainless steel, ceramic and synthetic sinks.
Tel: 0870 789 5107
www.leisure-sinks.co.uk

SINKS AND TAPS

WORKTOPS

BIZ ENGINEERING LTD
Zinc and stainless-steel sheets
sold cut to size or as made-to-
measure worktops.
Tel: 020 8443 3300

FORMICA
The Axiom range of surfaces
plus high-quality sheet laminates.
Tel: 0191 259 3512
www.formica-europe.com

GEC ANDERSON
Stylish and practical stainless-
steel worktops and sinks.
Tel: 01442 826999
www.gecanderson.co.uk

JUNCKERS
Solid hardwood for work
surfaces and floors.
Tel: 01376 534700
www.junckers.co.uk

ORAMA FABRICATIONS
Wide range of worktops in man-
made solid-surface materials.
Tel: 01773 520560
www.orama.co.uk

UK MARBLE
Marble, granite and stone
worktops made and installed.
Tel: 01432 352178
www.ukmarble.co.uk

SPLASHBACKS

AJ FABRICATIONS
Hi-tech aluminium treadplate
suitable for walls or floors.
Tel: 01483 276016

BRAGMAN FLETT
All types of metal, including
copper, brass, aluminium and
stainless steel.
Tel: 020 8337 1934

FIRED EARTH
Stylish plain and patterned wall
tiles, including handmade,
mosaic and glass designs.
Tel: 01295 814315
www.firedearth.com

H&R JOHNSON CERAMICS
Good choice of tiles, including
country-style designs with a
handcrafted appearance.
Tel: 01782 575575
www.johnson-tiles.com

MOSAIC WORKSHOP
Wide range of mosaic tiles, plus
products needed to apply them.
Tel: 020 7263 2997
www.mosaicworkshop.com

PILKINGTON'S CERAMIC TILES
Huge selection of ceramic tiles.
Tel: 0161 727 1111
www.pilkingtons.info

CARGO HOMESHOP
Dining furniture, affordable cookware and tableware. Sofas upholstered to order.
Tel: 01844 261800

THE CONRAN SHOP
Contemporary designer furniture, accessories, cookware and tableware.
Tel: 020 7589 7401
www.conran.co.uk

COURTS
Sofas, sofa beds, futons and other furniture.
Tel: 020 8640 3322
www.courts.co.uk

DUCAL
Solid wood furniture in classic designs; upholstered sofas.
Tel: 0870 742 9902
www.ducal-furniture.co.uk

ERCOL
Solid wood furniture including wood-framed sofas.
Tel: 01844 271800
www.ercol.com

FUTON COMPANY
Futon sofa beds and simple Japanese-style screens.
Tel: 0845 609 4455
www.futoncompany.co.uk

HIGHLY SPRUNG
Contemporary and traditional sofas and sofa beds.
Tel: 020 7924 1124
www.highlysprung.co.uk

THE IRON DESIGN COMPANY
Handmade iron sofas, tables and chairs. Can also make pieces to customers' own specifications.
Tel: 01609 778143
www.irondesign.co.uk

LLOYD LOOM OF SPALDING
Woven fibre furniture, including the classic Lloyd Loom chairs.
Tel: 01775 712111
www.lloydloom.com

THE LOOSE COVER COMPANY
Loose sofa and chair covers made to order.
Tel: 01494 471226

MAGNET
Fitted and freestanding furniture in a range of styles.
01325 744344
www.magnet.co.uk

MFI
Affordable furniture in solid pine and other wood finishes.
Tel: 0800 028 0937
www.mfi.co.uk

MULTIYORK
Custom-made sofas, sofa beds
and chairs, with thousands of
upholstery fabrics to choose
from; wooden cabinet furniture.
Tel: 0870 527 3747
www.multiyork.co.uk

OCEAN
Contemporary shelving
units and wheeled coffee
tables in beech and maple;
leather sofas.
Tel: 01993 770435
www.oceanuk.com

THE PIER
Ethnic-style furniture ranges,
many in dark wood or bamboo.
Tel: 0845 609 1234
www.pier.co.uk

PURVES & PURVES
Innovative designer furniture,
including Italian sofas.
Tel: 020 7580 8223 for stockists;
020 8993 2064 for mail order
www.purves.co.uk

SCUMBLE GOOSIE
Ready-to-paint wooden furniture
and screens in classic designs.
Tel: 01453 731315
www.scumble-goosie.co.uk

SHAKER
Wooden furniture mostly in
cherry or maple; peg rails, oval
boxes and other Shaker-style
furnishings and accessories.
Tel: 020 7935 9461
www.shaker.co.uk

SOFA WORKSHOP
Wide range of sofas, including
contemporary, classic and
leather designs.
Tel: 01798 343400 for stockists
01443 238699 for mailorder
www.sofaworkshopdirect.co.uk
www.sofaworkshop.com

VIVA SOFA
Contemporary sofas and chairs,
including leather designs.
Tel: 01443 239444
www.vivasofa.co.uk

AMAZING GRATES
Reproduction period fireplaces.
Tel: 020 8883 5556

ELGIN & HALL
Made-to-order fireplaces
in a wide range of styles.
Tel: 01677 450100
www.elgin.co.uk

PECO
Vast choice of doors and
fully restored fireplaces.
Tel: 020 8979 8310

WICKES
Fires and fire surrounds; glass
blocks for partition walls.
Tel: 0500 300 328
www.wickes.co.uk

WINTHER BROWNE
Simple fire surrounds in pine,
mahogany and MDF; flatpack
ready-to-paint radiator cabinets.
Tel: 020 8803 3434

FIREPLACES AND FITTINGS

CROWN PAINTS
Vast choice, including the mix-
to-order Expressions collection.
Tel: 01254 704951
www.crownpaint.co.uk

DULUX
Vast choice of shades in many
ranges, including the extensive
Colour Mixing System.
Tel: 01753 550555
www.dulux.co.uk

FARROW & BALL
Heritage paint shades.
Tel: 01202 876141
www.farrow-ball.co.uk

HOMEBASE
Wide choice, including ranges by
Jane Churchill and Laura Ashley.
Tel: 0870 900 8098
www.homebase.co.uk

INTERNATIONAL PAINT
Paints and primers for
melamine, radiators and floors.
Tel: 01480 484284
www.plascon.co.uk

PLASTI-KOTE
Decorative spray paints,
including metallics.
Tel: 01223 836400
www.spraypaint.co.uk

PAINTS

DECORATIVE EFFECTS

THE ENGLISH STAMP COMPANY
Wall stamps and stamping tools.
Tel: 01929 439117
www.englishstamp.com

HOMECRAFTS DIRECT
Craft products by mail order.
Tel: 0116 269 7733
www.homecrafts.co.uk

HUMBROL
Makers of Glass Etch spray
that creates a frosted effect
on glass.
Tel: 01482 701191

LIBERON
Waxes and other wood finishes.
Tel: 01797 367555

PÉBÉO
Fabric, china and porcelain
paints and pens.
Tel: 02380 701144
www.pebeo.com

RONSEAL
Paint & Grain kits, melamine
paints and woodcare products.
Tel: 0114 246 7171
www.ronseal.co..uk

FABRICS AND WALLPAPERS

CATH KIDSTON
Retro 1950s-style floral cottons.
Tel: 020 7221 4000 for stockists
020 7229 8000 for mail order.
www.cathkidston.co.uk

COLOROLL
Contemporary wallcoverings
and coordinating fabrics.
Tel: 0800 056 4878
www.coloroll.co.uk

COLEFAX & FOWLER
Florals on linen and chintz, and
complementary wallpapers.
Tel: 020 8877 6400

CROWN WALLCOVERINGS & HOME FURNISHINGS
Wide range of wallcoverings.
Tel: 0800 458 1554
www.ihdg.co.uk

DESIGNERS GUILD
Colourful contemporary fabrics,
wallpapers and paints.
Tel: 020 7351 5775
www.designersguild.com

GRAHAM & BROWN
Contemporary wallcoverings,
including textures and metallics.
Tel: 0800 3288452
www.grahambrown.com

IAN MANKIN
Natural fabrics in plains, stripes and checks, including plenty of classic tickings and ginghams.
Tel: 020 7722 0997

KNICKERBEAN
Discount stores with designer fabrics at bargain prices.
Tel: 01842 751327

THE NATURAL FABRIC COMPANY
Wide range of natural fabrics.
Tel: 01488 684002

OSBORNE & LITTLE
Classic and contemporary prints, weaves and wallpapers.
Tel: 020 7352 1456
www.osborneandlittle.com

SANDERSON
Coordinated fabric and wallcovering ranges.
Tel: 01895 830044
www.sanderson-uk.com

WILMAN INTERIORS
Contemporary and classic fabrics and wallpapers.
Tel: 01282 727300
www.wilman.co.uk

THE CURTAIN EXCHANGE
Quality secondhand curtains bought and sold.
Tel: 020 7731 8316
www.thecurtainexchange.cwc.net

LUXAFLEX
Made-to-measure blinds.
Tel: 0800 652779
www.luxaflex.com

PRÊT À VIVRE
Curtains and blinds made to measure; poles and tiebacks.
Tel: 0845 1305161
www.pretavivre.com

ROSEBYS
Ready-made curtains and blinds.
Tel: 0800 052 0493
www.rosebys.com

RUFFLETTE
Tiebacks, blind and eyelet kits and curtain-making products.
Tel: 0161 998 1811
www.rufflette.com

THE SHUTTER SHOP
Wooden shutters made to order; wooden Venetian blinds.
Tel: 01252 844575
www.shuttershop.co.uk

WINDOW TREATMENTS

FLOORING

ALLIED CARPETS
Carpet superstores with a huge range of colours and patterns.
Tel: 01689 895000

AMTICO
Quality vinyl flooring, including wood, stone and glass effects.
Tel: 0800 667766
www.amtico.com

BRINTONS
Vast range of Axminster and Wilton carpets.
Tel: 0800 505055
www.brintons.co.uk

CRUCIAL TRADING
Natural floorcoverings and rugs in sisal, coir and seagrass.
Tel: 01562 743747
www.crucial-trading.com

DALSOUPLE
Rubber flooring in many colours.
Tel: 01278 727733
www.dalsouple.com

FORBO-NAIRN
Practical flooring, including Cushionflor vinyl and natural product Marmoleum.
Tel: 01592 643777
www.nairn-cushionflor.co.uk

HARVEY MARIA
PVC laminated floor tiles with funky photographic images.
Tel: 020 8516 7788
www.harveymaria.co.uk

PERGO ORIGINAL
Wood-effect laminate flooring.
Tel: 0800 374771
www.pergo.com

RICHARD BURBIDGE
Wood-effect laminate boards that click together for easy fitting.
Tel: 01691 678201
www.richardburbidge.co.uk

RYALUX CARPETS
Wool carpets that can be supplied in any width.
Tel: 0800 163632
www.ryalux.carpetinfo.co.uk

STONELL
Stone tiles, including limestone, sandstone and slate.
Tel: 01892 833500
www.stonell.com

WICANDERS
High-quality wood and cork flooring in many finishes.
Tel: 01403 710001
www.wicanders.com

BHS
Stylish but affordable lights and shades in a range of styles.
Tel: 020 7262 3288
www.bhs.co.uk

BISQUE RADIATORS
Designer-style radiators in many shapes, sizes and finishes.
Tel: 01225 478500
www.bisque.co.uk

CHRISTOPHER WRAY LIGHTING
Huge range of designs, from cutting-edge to traditional.
Tel: 020 7751 8701
www.christopher-wray.com

JOHN CULLEN LIGHTING
Discreet downlighters, spots and uplighters for creating atmospheric effects.
Tel: 020 7371 5400

MATHMOS
Lava lamps in many shapes, sizes and colours.
Tel: 020 7549 2700
www.mathmos.com

MCCLOUD & CO
Vast choice of light fittings by British craftspeople, available in a selection of different finishes.
Tel: 020 7352 1533
www.mccloud.co.uk

THE RADIATOR COMPANY
Stylish radiators in traditional and modern designs.
Tel: 01342 302250
www.theradiatorcompany.co.uk

RYNESS ELECTRICAL SUPPLIES
Well-made light fittings, including recessed eyeball ceiling lights.
Tel: 020 7278 8993
www.ryness.co.uk

SKK LIGHTS
Innovative light fittings, including some wacky designs.
Tel: 020 7434 4095
www.skk.net

THE STIFFKEY LAMPSHOP
Original and reproduction lamps, candlesticks and candelabra.
Tel: 01328 830460

LIGHTING AND HEATING

ACCESSORIES

ALESSI
Stylish modern kitchenware,
including quirky accessories in
colourful moulded plastic.
Tel: 020 7518 9091
www.alessi.com

BOMBAY DUCK
Decorative contemporary
accessories, including photo
frames and beaded items.
Tel: 020 8749 8001
www.bombayduck.co.uk

DIVERTIMENTI
Practical and stylish tableware,
cookware and small appliances.
Tel: 020 7935 0689
www.divertimenti.co.uk

FOUND
Candleholders, cushions, picture
frames and other accessories, to
complement both classic and
contemporary looks.
Tel: 0800 316 8121
www.foundat.co.uk

LAKELAND LIMITED
Practical cookware, gadgets and
storage accessories.
Tel: 01539 488100
www.lakelandlimited.co.uk

MONSOON HOME
Embroidered throws and
cushions in colourful silks.
Tel: 020 7313 3000
www.monsoon.co.uk

SIA
Wide range of small accessories
designed to complement popular
decorating themes.
Tel: 0870 608 6060

SUMMERILL & BISHOP
Old and new kitchenware from
around the world.
Tel: 020 7221 4566

T&G WOODWARE
Wood, marble and melamine
kitchenware, and wooden trolleys.
Tel: 01275 841841
www.tg-woodware.co.uk

WAX LYRICAL
Decorative candles and
candleholders.
Tel: 01229 469600

THE CARPET FOUNDATION
Free booklets giving advice on
choosing and caring for carpets.
Tel: 01562 755568
www.carpetfoundation.com

COUNCIL FOR REGISTERED
GAS INSTALLERS (CORGI)
All gas installers must be CORGI
registered. The Council can
recommend one in your area.
Tel: 01256 372200

THE KITCHEN SPECIALISTS'
ASSOCIATION
Can supply lists of reputable
kitchen design companies. Free
leaflets available on what to look
out for when buying a kitchen.
Tel: 01905 726066

THE LIGHTING ASSOCIATION
Advice on where to find answers
to lighting queries; free buyers'
guide available.
Tel: 01952 290905
www.lightingassociation.com

NATIONAL ASSOCIATION OF
PLUMBING, HEATING AND
MECHANICAL SERVICES
CONTRACTORS
Can supply lists of members and
advice on plumbing and heating.
Tel: 024 7647 0626
www.licensedplumber.co.uk

NATIONAL FIREPLACE
ASSOCIATION
General information on
fireplaces and fuels.
Tel: 0121 200 1310
www.nfa.org.uk

NATIONAL INSPECTION
COUNCIL FOR ELECTRICAL
INSTALLATION CONTRACTING
Can supply lists of electricians,
free leaflets and advice.
Tel: 020 7564 2323

THE PAINTERS AND
DECORATORS ASSOCIATION
Can supply a list of decorators
in your area and a leaflet
advising how to choose one.
Tel: 02476 353776;
www.paintingdecoratingassocia-
tion.co.uk

THE ROYAL INSTITUTE OF
BRITISH ARCHITECTS
Can send out lists of member
architects in your area.
Tel: 020 7580 5533
www.architecture.com

NATIONAL INSTITUTE OF
CARPET AND FLOOR LAYERS
Help with finding the right
professionals to fit flooring.
Tel: 0115 958 3077
www.nicfltd.org.uk

ADVICE